ASTROLOGY UNCUT

ROB MARRIOTT
AND SONYA MAGETT

ONE WORLD
BALLANTINE
NEW YORK

ASTROLOGY
UNCUT

A
STREET-SMART
GUIDE
TO THE STARS

A ONE WORLD BOOK

Published by The Random House Publishing Group

Copyright © 2004 by Rob Marriott and Sonya Magett

One World and Ballantine are registered trademarks and the
One World colophon is a trademark of Random House, Inc.

www.ballantinebooks.com/one

The Library of Congress Control Number is available upon request.

ISBN 0-8129-6793-3

Manufactured in the United States of America

First Edition: March 2004

10 9 8 7 6 5 4 3 2 1

Book design by Barbara M. Bachman

Zodiac illustrations by Glenn "Elf" Fletcher

To my mother—
your great sense of style and creative writing
inspired my passion for fashion and publishing.

—S.M.

For my sister Kimica—
my first study in Cancer/Leo.

—R.M.

It's a game we all play. Whether you check your horoscope daily, think the whole astrology thing is some ol' bullshit, or grudgingly admit to seeing some truth in it, categorizing friends, enemies, and in-betweens by their star signs is a global pastime. Absolutely everyone can be located along the cosmic dial. Everyone, no matter the race, class, sexual preference, number of legs, amount of gold teeth, or how many shoes you bought last week. It's a universal thing, which might account for astrology's ever-growing popularity, especially among the post–hip-hop generation.

So the theory goes that the lady Virgo (August 24 to September 22) passes down a quiet, sometimes fanatic perfectionism to all her chill'un; that Scorpios (October 23–November 21) all share a demonic capacity for possessiveness; that those born under the sign of Aries the Ram (March 21–April 19), no matter what their station in life, all got fire in their blood; and so on. And from there the game begins. First the questions: Is it true about me? My man? My mother?

Where a lot of people get dismissive about astrology is this idea that the stars predetermine your life. Nah. Not that simple. Real astrol-ogy (not that bullshit psychic network nonsense) speaks to your tendencies, identifies the certain energies coursing through your body that make you more likely to fight (Aries) or flee (Pisces) or whatever. Look at it this way: the zodiac affects your psyche the way genetics affects your body. You are given a certain set of talents and weaknesses under a certain set of conditions, which will be explained later in this chapter. This set of conditions teaches us lessons that develop our souls. That's it. From that point, what you do with what you got is on you, playa.

Many still dismiss astrology as a cheap device that clowns with no game use to try and push up on females at a club. (How did Biggie put it? *Who they attractin' with that line/what's your name? What's your sign?*) We who have a real understanding of the influence of the stars and planets see it a different way. This is knowledge that has come down through the ages. This is insight. This is what's *really* happenin', underneath all the facades and deceptions and game.

Astrologers have been consulted throughout history by kings, queens, and military leaders to determine their next move, be it the fate of nations or that next vacation. Napoleon, Chinese emperors, kings of England, all consulted with astrologers. Nancy Reagan, wife of the former president, was on it so hard she supposedly wouldn't allow the president to make a move unless it was astrologically okayed. Don't get it twisted. Astrology is more than the bullshit horoscopes in a newspaper. It has more influence on our lives than we even know. The real appeal of astrology is the idea that there's actually some order underlining all the chaos in our lives.

Trying to get a grip on what motivates the people in our lives to do the things they do is a full-time job with no benefits. No dental, nothing. Struggling to understand their actions, we find ourselves asking the age-old questions like: *Who does that heifer think she is? Or Is this motherfucker tryin' to play me?* And so on. In this respect, astrology can help. Perhaps knowing that said heifer is Leo and has nothing against you personally might help put things into perspective. Or recognizing that the aforementioned motherfucker is a Capricorn who makes others suffer only because he is silently suffering himself might make the situation a little easier to fathom. Possibly. We make no promises.

Still, even a vague familiarity with astrology can up your situation-handling abilities greatly. It can provide clarity when faced with that looming drama awaiting you in your hood. It might explain why your cousin got all Rasheed Wallace at the dinner table last week. And it miiight be just the thing when dealing with the babymommadrama. True, astrology can't help you with that upcoming court case or that money you owe Pookie Doo or that hefty car note, but what it can tell you is why the fuck you purchased a Lexus on your barely-making-it salary in the first place (see Libra, page 67).

But this ain't encyclopedia astrologica. Not supposed to be. This is an itty-bitty sun sign book, the tip of the iceberg when it comes to what astrology actually has to offer. Think of this as just an intro to everything you ever wanted to know about signs but was too to'e up on Hypnotiq to bother asking. In other words, this is astrology customized for the MTV-addicted post–hip-hop generation, written for the edification of attention-deficient maufuckas like yourselves.

Customized? Yes, to make things perfectly clear and accessible, this is a record of astrology at work in the ghettocentric ferment. Also known as urban culture. Yeah, exactly. Tupac Shakur (Gemini). Twenty-four-inch rims (Taurus). James Bond (Scorpio). Pamela Anderson (Cancer). Prada bags (Virgo). Bruce Lee (Sagittarius). Batman (Scorpio). Pit bulls (Sagittarius). Sunflower seeds (Leo). Court-appointed lawyers (Libra). Ghetto booty queen J.Lo (Leo). *Grand Theft Auto* (Aries). iPods (Aquarius). Scarface, the movie and the rapper (Taurus and Scorpio, respectively). We can go on and on. Everything carefully placed in its appropriate spot along the cosmic dial. All laid out for our ongoing game of compare and contrast.

Just think about it for a second: doesn't Mike Tyson's lunacy make more sense when you know his ruling planet is the moon (see Cancer, page 33)? Wouldn't it be a comfort to Virgos to know that fellow Virgo Beyoncé Knowles, despite her superstar status and fame (or bootyliciousness), still struggles with security issues? Would it not fill you with Scorpio pride to realize that you have something profoundly in common with the Ol' Dirty Bastard himself? Okay, maybe not. But you see what we gettin' at. More important, if used right, astrology is a guide to self-understanding.

So say no more, praise Jesus. The wait is over. Thank the Lord. *Astrology Uncut* is heah to provide salvation to the confused, wayward, and game-deprived. Now let us bow our heads and read.

Contents

THE JUMP OFF

The study of the positions and aspects of heavenly bodies in the belief that they have influence on the course of human affairs.

We are not talking that vague-ass daily horoscope shit. This is a book about basic sun-sign astrology, which is a science. See, back in the days, scholars and scientists in ancient societies understood the universe as a vast and infinite union. In their cosmology, nothing was separate. Everything was everything. The birth of a human being was considered a manifestation of that moment in the space-time continuum. Astrology sees us as a reflection of the moment based on the position of planets in the solar system. In other words, we take on the traits of that moment in time. Hence, folk born in the summer have "summertime" dispositions (outgoing, gregarious, hot-blooded), while winter children are more reflective of the colder months (internal, detached, cool). The sky was divided into twelve, and the energies of those twelve periods were named, identified, and documented. The influences of heavenly bodies were also documented. Some believe the three kings in the Christmas story were all learned in astrology, which is why they knew where and when the Christ child would be born, and that the star they followed was actually a number of planets in a rare alignment, a foretold sign of the messiah's birth.

An astrological chart is like a blueprint to a soul. To the trained astrologer, looking at a chart of the exact configuration of the planets in the sky when a person was born is like reading his or her FBI files.

IN YA FACE ASTROLOGY:

This is our approach to the zodiac as seen through the filter of the post–hip-hop ghettocentric experience. *Astrology Uncut* is a synthesis of understandings. It is what other books are afraid to tell you, spoken in a language we can all understand, without all the polite wineglass clinking or new-agey hippie nonsense.

So now that we've defined our approach, let's break the zodiac down. Break it down to its very last compound. The twelve signs can be categorized along these lines:

- masculine or feminine
- fixed, cardinal, or mutable
- element (fire, earth, air, or water)
- axis
- ruling planet

MASCULINE/FEMININE

The masculine signs are the yang signs of the zodiac: more forward-looking and initiating, more aggressive and instigating. Air and fire signs are masculine.

The feminine signs are the yin signs of the zodiac: more passive and indirect, more accepting and flowing. Earth and water signs are feminine.

FIXED/CARDINAL/MUTABLE

The fixed signs are power signs. Not easily swayed, these four signs—Taurus, Scorpio, Leo, and Aquarius—are at ease in the driver's seat. They are marked by their utter determination that their will be done. They set standards and usually become the deciding factor in any social situation.

The cardinal signs are the initiating signs, the ones that begin the four seasons: Aries (spring), Cancer (summer), Libra (fall), and Capricorn (winter). They are marked by leadership abilities and the innate capacity to transform themselves.

The mutable signs are quick-change artists and fluid maneuverers. So quick to move, they can be led astray if the current is strong enough. Gemini, Virgo, Sagittarius, and Pisces all work from a sensitivity to their surroundings and an ability to respond and react intensely. But while Pisces and Virgo might instinctively fall back from a situation, Sagittarius and Gemini react by stepping forward.

THE ELEMENTS

Fire Signs: Dons and Divas

The three fire signs are Aries, Leo, and Sagittarius. Basically, they want attention by any means necessary. Brilliant at times, they can be hot or cool, beautiful or destructive. They bore easily, so they stay on the go. Their solution is to find pleasure in variety. They're not really the settling-down type. They can be relentless and demanding. Take an accounting of the real divas of the last century—Diana, Aretha, Billie, Whitney—

LIKE MOST FIRE-SIGN PERSONALITIES, LEO DIVA MADONNA DOES WHATEVER THE HELL SHE WANTS.

and it is all fire signs, all day. If they can get you on the defensive, it's a wrap. Persistent and fast-moving, fire signs *move* like fire, burning through any- and everything with little thought of who gets charred. This is the realm of instinct. Fire-sign cats seem lucky, if only because they've been blessed with a powerful instinct and an optimistic, forward-looking mentality.

Fire-sign development begins with Aries, the wild ram-child, presenting itself with boldness and without self-consciousness. That attention-craving energy evolves into Leo, the prideful and regal lion, brimming with confidence and ambition. Sagittarius, the centaur, half beast and half man, concludes the trajectory, turning fiery ambition into spiritual initiation.

Earth Signs: Keepin' It Very Real

The three earth signs are Taurus, Virgo, and Capricorn. Possessive, practical, hard-working, and tolerating little nonsense, earth signs exemplify the phrase "gettin' good with real." They rule the material world and progressively represent the evolution of material possessions. It starts with Taurus, the bull, who has a talent for and an inclination toward amassing wealth and material things. Virgo, the maiden, with a critical eye ana-

CAPRICORN LL COOL J HAS THE STAYING POWER TYPICAL OF EARTH SIGNS.

lyzes the material, measuring and calculating in preparation for using it. That is where Capricorn, the goat-fish, comes in. Caps understand how to use the material to get the most out of it. And that they do very well.

The thing about earth signs is they try to have that ass on lock! They think they own you, everything they bought you, and everything you bought for yourself. So security-minded and risk-averse that sometimes they might not move. So much so that life can pass them by. Can get complacent at times. Stuck in a rut if they're not careful. It's a security thing. All decisions are made for the long run. Stable, re-liable, they do things by the book.

GEMINI CHE GUEVARA, LIKE MOST AIR-SIGNS PERSONAL-ITIES, WAS AN INTELLECTUAL REVOLUTIONARY FIGHTING FOR CHANGE.

Air Signs: Beatin' You in the Head

Air signs are all about making connec-tions. The three air signs are Gemini, Libra, and Aquarius. These folks have greedy minds in constant need of stim-ulation—so much so that they will con-coct scenarios to make things more, uh . . . stimulating (if you get the drift). Like fire signs, air signs are constantly moving, but in a different manner. Com-munication, socialization, and experi-mentation are the modes in which air signs create their own stimulus.

Gemini, the twin souls in perpetual conversation, initiates the electric realm of air and ideas—Geminis are quick-moving and talkative, and their forward-thinking movements turn into the calculation of the criminal-minded Libra. The Libra symbol, the scales of justice, represents the building of society. Aquarius, the sky-born man pouring down the waters of celestial information, concludes the air movement by living the principle that knowledge will unite humanity.

Water Signs: You Feel Me?

The three water signs are Cancer, Scorpio, and Pisces. These sensitive-ass feeling-e'erything motherfuckers can get on your nerves or can save your life. Or both. Ooh, so secretive! The deeper the water, the less you know about them. Cancer introduces the realm of emotion into the zodiac. In contrast to the initiative of fire, the intellectualizing of air, and the materialism of earth, water signs demonstrate both the blessing and curse when it comes to emotions. Cancer's nur-

CANCER O. J. SIMPSON'S HIGHLY EMOTIONAL COURT CASE IS ONE EXAMPLE OF HOW DEEP IT CAN GET FOR WATER-SIGN PERSONALITIES.

turing and fluidlike changeability (moodiness) turn into Scorpio's manipulation and volatility. Scorpio comes with the focus to direct emotional energy like a leather whip. In the last of the water signs, Pisces, after releasing all of the pent-up energy and emotion of Scorpio, the soul simply lets go. In this zodiac, emotions (specifically love) become the vehicle to the next level/dimension/soul session. Which can be a good or a bad thing, mind you.

THE AXIS POWERS

Some astrologers say that there are actually only six signs in the zodiac, and two sides to each of them. In truth, the axes (otherwise known as opposites) are karmically linked. Study the traits of any single zodiac sign and the latent elements of the opposite sign can be easily seen.

Aries-Libra Axis

Impulse and indecision, initiation and balance. This axis gets what it wants by any means necessary. While the Aries will tantrum till its needs are met, the Libra will smile you to death, take away all your inhibitions, and convince you with all the charm in the world that what you want is really what he/she wants. It's only much later that you realize you been macked.

Taurus-Scorpio Axis

The focus: Money, sex, and power. Money, sex, and power. Taureans Master P and Busta Rhymes, Scorpios Eve and P. Diddy, all came to prominence during the bling-bling era. These are the folks that cele-brate champagne, platinum, and shiny cars as if they were born with silver spoons in their mouths. These are also the folks who are known for their twenty-four-hour work schedules. Coincidence? We think not. This axis is about havin' thangs, then usin' them for everything they're worth. What makes this axis so powerful is that while Taurus rules ac-quisition, Scorpio masters it. Greed might be the only thing that can undo this powerful axis.

Gemini-Sagittarius Axis

These are characters. Eclectic, fashion-conscious, daring. Instigators and salesmen. Always conduits of information. These cats keep it thoroughly comic book. Their escapades are wild, with outfits to match. These are the master communicators: Gemini does it with a trickster's smirk, Sag does it with a gangster's swagger. Both will bite their tongue for no one. Both are dual-natured and use their split per-sonalities to tag-team unsuspecting victims. With Gemini it's good cop and bad cop rolled into one. With Sagittarius it's a caring, gregarious teacher vs. a bold animal driven by pure instinct. Both are extremely dangerous. HANDLE WITH CARE. These folk can and will run mental circles around your ass if you're not careful.

Cancer-Capricorn Axis

Emotions run real deep here. Sensitive. Moody. Joy and pain, sunshine and rain. Cancer's ever-changing moods become Capricorn's deep, dark stillness and coldness, but don't be fooled. Beneath the surface, Capricorns are as deeply emotional and internally fluctuating as Cancers; they just hide it better. The folk on this axis suffer emotionally, so the Cancer distracts herself with sex, baubles, and children, the Capricorn with work and money. One could almost call this the mother/father axis. Cancer comes with a caring softness, while Capricorns are stern, sometimes cruel disciplinarians.

Leo-Aquarius Axis

Visionaries. Futuristic. Action and intellect. A beautiful example of the Leo-Aquarius axis is Bob Marley's song "War." The vision of a borderless world and a united humanity is in keeping with the Aquarian ideal. The Leo king of Ethiopia, Haile Selassie, gave a speech and Aquarius Marley adapted it and spread its message throughout the world in song. The

TRIFE LIFE:
AQUARIAN BOBBY
BROWN AND LEO
WHITNEY HOUSTON

boldness of the statement is in keeping with Leo leadership. (Not that this axis can't be trifling too. Aquarius Bobby Brown and Leo Whitney Houston are another example of what this axis is capable of.) The power of this axis comes from uniting people. The Leo attracts them with a showman's flair and the Aquarian organizes them under the principles of unity. When heading in the wrong direction, however, this axis can be a destructive force.

Virgo-Pisces Axis

Sacrifice and analysis. Dreams and reality. These two signs represent the infinite reaches, wisdom and intuition from beyond. The blessing and the burden. As with Cancer-Capricorn, emotions run deep here, too. The Virgo-Pisces axis tends to make major sacrifices for loved ones. Virgo is the vessel for spiritual wisdom, the earthbound body it comes through. Pisceans are ancient souls ready to be unburdened of this earthly body. The best representation of this axis is the Madonna and child—the Madonna, of course, representing the Virgin (Virgo symbol) and the child representing the Christ (who some believe is a Pisces).

THE PLANETS

Sun

Ruler of Leo, and the most influential of the heavenly bodies. The sun determines your modus operandi, your rhythm, your physicality, how you move through the world.

Moon

Ruler of the emotional realm. The moon rules Cancer and puts the sign through severe mood changes monthly. As the moon goes through its phases, so does Cancer. It also gives Cancer powerful intuition.

Mercury

This planet was named after a messenger of the gods who served as go-between for the heavens and humanity. Mercury rules communications, gadgets, electricity, short trips, and mental processes. Gemini and Virgo are ruled by Mercury, making them quick thinkers and very articulate—in Gemini's case, overarticulate. It's why oftentimes these two signs are so compatible.

Venus

The planet of love and beauty. This planet rules how the signs under its influence give of themselves. It also graces the zodiac signs it rules, Taurus and Libra, with a certain attractiveness.

Mars

The war planet, or planet of aggression. It was named after a god of war. It rules Aries and Scorpio, both of which are very dangerous opponents if you ever get into beef with either of them.

Jupiter

The king planet, gregarious and considered both lucky and generous. Jupiter rules Sagittarius and gives this sign an affable, good-time demeanor. Santa's a Sag.

Saturn

The planet of limitation and restriction. It rules Capricorn and Aquarius. Saturn gives both signs an air of detachment and cool reserve. Saturn can be so restrictive as to stifle all movement. Caps in particular are susceptible to arthritis.

Uranus

The planet of sudden change and revolution. It also rules the sign of Aquarius, the iconoclast of the zodiac. Uranus represents the lightning bolt, which is both inspiration and destruction.

Neptune

The planet of dreams and illusions. Pisces, which is ruled by Neptune, lives in a world of dreams. Neptune also brings a spiritual nature to Pisces and an extreme sensitivity.

Pluto

The dark planet, sign of mystery and cataclysmic change. It gives Scorpio a dark, powerful energy that builds slowly and then explodes with unprecedented force. Not to be played with.

In every chapter we've provided a "rundown" on each sign, which we've defined for you on the following page.

THE RUNDOWN

Motto	*karmic direction*
Sound bite	*what's likely to come out of their mouth*
Ruling planet	*self-explanatory*
Color	*ditto*
Rock	*birthstone*
Physical	*ruling body part*
Icon	*representative figure*
Genius	*exemplary figure of the sign's astrological gifts*
Beverage	*what cats is drinkin'*
Guilty pleasure	*secret sin*
Accessory	*the must-have*
Ride	*what cats is drivin'*
Find them	*the usual spot/activity*
Visual	*movie, video, or image*
Moment	*the zodiac sign in its full manifestation*
Street occupation/grind	*moneymaking endeavor*
Mix tape	*music by and for cats born under the sign*
Best-case scenario	*self-explanatory*
Worst-case scenario	*ditto*
Spot	*location with the same astrology*
Erogenous zone	*where they're likely to bang it out*
Vice	*likely flaw*
Natural talent	*likely gifts*
Compatibilities	*who they wit'?*

THE GHETTO INDEX

Each chapter also features a Ghetto Index for the sign, which measures the capacity to survive and thrive in the shantyvilles of urban America. This index is not cut along racial lines, although the burden of skin color in this society might make you more susceptible to ghetto inclinations. Ghetto, as we look at it, is a combination of mental fitness, trifeness, and survival skills. We break down the index into nine indicators: Gangstability, Booty quotient, Bling quotient, Drama quotient, Don status, Trick status, Game quotient, Shiest quotient, and Freak quotient. All aspects transcend ghetto life, but all are particularly necessary in a struggling urban environment.

Take booty, for example. Booty (or ass, to get right down to it) is really a signifier of sexuality. As for the individual rating, we explain it like this. Sarah Michelle Gellar might be pretty and attractive in a Hollywood context, but Ms. Gellar, despite all of her other graces, got no ass. No love in the hood. That's guaranteed. Halle Berry gets higher ratings, of course, but still she is high middlin' in regard to booty matters. Trina, on the other hand, gets high honors on the booty scale. She's packing. Serena Williams? Off the charts.

Rating	1-4	5-7	8-10
Gangstability	*bitch-ass*	*holdin' they own*	*can't fuck wit'*
Booty quotient	*no ass*	*onion*	*badoonkadoonk*
Bling quotient	*Black Thought*	*Jay-Z*	*Liberace*
Drama quotient	*off-Broadway*	*Hollywood*	*DJ Kay Slay mix tape*
Don status	*Knotts*	*King*	*Corleone*
Trick status	*pay for a drink*	*takin' 'em shopping*	*turns ho into housewife*
Game quotient	*monopoly*	*chess*	*drug*
Shiest quotient	*snitch*	*sleeping with the enemy*	*letting your momma take the fall*
Freak quotient	*Dr. Ruth*	*Lil' Kim*	*Janet Jacme*

So it goes with all the indicators. But if you still don't get it, we devised a handy little reference chart (see above) for your convenience.

High score on the index suggests real trifeness. Low score on the index indicates high likelihood of gettin' ganked, victimized, or the like. Get it? Got it? Good. If not, call somebody or figure as you go, 'cause explainin' time is over. Let's get to it.

A S T R O L O G Y **U N C U T**

WANNA BE
STARTIN'
SUMTHIN':
ARIES LIKE SUGE DEMAN
THAT YOU RESPECT THEI
GANGSTA. OR ELSE.

ARIES 03.21–04.19

BITCH BETTA HAVE MY BOTTLE

THE RUNDOWN

masculine, *cardinal, fire*

Motto *I am*

Sound bite *"What's mine is mine and what's yours is mine"*

Ruling planet *Mars*

Color *red*

Rock *diamond*

Physical *head*

Icon *Popeye; Redman logo*

Genius *Eddie Murphy*

Beverage *red quarter water*

Guilty pleasure *starting fights*

Accessory *blunt object*

Ride *Ducati motorcycle*

Find them *at a boxing match*

Visual The Harder They Come; Set It Off

Moment *Carmen Electra marries Dennis Rodman*

THE RUNDOWN

Street occupation/grind *the muscle; gorilla pimp*

Mix tape *Juvenile, "400 Degreez"; Chaka Khan, "Through the Fire"; Redman, "I'll Bee Dat!"; Q-Tip, "Vivrant Thing"; De La Soul, "Me Myself and I"; Marvin Gaye, "Here, My Dear"; Aretha Franklin, "Rock Steady"; Pharrell of the Neptunes, "Frontin'"*

Best-case scenario *Aretha Franklin*

Worst-case scenario *Suge Knight*

Spot *Baghdad*

Erogenous zone *your momma's bed*

Vice *getting in static*

Natural talent *getting over*

Compatibilities *Gemini, Leo, Libra*

ASTROLOGY UNCUT

GHETTO INDEX

Gangstability	9	
Booty quotient	7	
Bling quotient	7	
Drama quotient	10	
Don status	5	
Trick status	2	
Game quotient	5	
Shiest quotient	3	
Freak quotient	7	

Aries folk are what you might call provocateurs. Ram types love an argument. A beatdown? Even better. Up for any challenge, any opponent, any time, anywhere: *whu, nigga, what?* Real rah-rah. The trigger first, politic later type. Ruled by the planet Mars, these fire-sign personalities are hot-blooded to a fault and not afraid of banging heads with somebody. Understand: this is how rams communicate. It is also how they read a situation: to see what they can get away with. As in saying some off-the-wall shit like "You always acting like a bitch" and seeing what happens. It's why Aries director and quintessential white boy Quentin Tarantino felt the need to say "nigger" four thousand times in his movie *Pulp Fiction.* Juuust testing.

Aries demand that you respect their gangsta. *Will* whoop that ass, if pressed. Thrive in conflict. Believe that. Remember when Da Brat got accused of pistol-whipping some woman in Atlanta? We ain't saying she's guilty, but that's some real Aries shit right dere. Want a vivid example of the Aries temperament? Three words: Marion "Suge" Knight. Let's

NATURAL GENIUS: ARIES LIKE EDDIE MURPHY BALANCE OUT THEIR BOISTEROUS WAYS WITH OVERLOADS OF CHARISMA AND TALENT.

5

ARIES

not even talk about all the blood-soaked stories about cats getting their heads beaten in with champagne bottles, or forced to strip in bathroom stalls, or hung from balconies. Suge is Aries from head to toe. Meteoric rise to fame and fortune marked by impulse and violence, all the red suits, big-ass diamonds shining from both lobes. Think about it: Suge is a war-minded alpha male who terrorized an industry for years and left carnage in his wake. But his momma nicknamed him "Sugar Bear." Warmonger and momma's boy? That's Aries all day.

To truly understand the Aries personality is to recognize that no matter how old they get, they remain, at their core, infants. Babies are cute, magnetic, and, unless moms was smokin' that crack or something, bursting with life. So it goes with Aries. It's why Aries celebrities dub themselves with infantile names like Da Brat and Babyface. Think Redman, hip-hop's preeminent Aries manchild, and his enfant terrible logo. Aries, in fact, are wonderful as children. Because they are in their natural age range, they glow with a special light.

Every sign has a natural age: Aries is the infant. Taurus is the toddler. Gemini represents the age when a child learns to talk and communicate. Cancer is an emotional preteen, and Leo comes with the arrogance of adolescence. Virgo is the young adult. Libra is the age most people get married and fully enter society. Scorpio is the second childhood of the thirties, Sagittarius the expansive forties. Capricorn is the power and prestige that come with the fifties. Aquarius is the

> **wisdom that comes in the seventies. And Pisces is the quiet end of life, where the childlike aspects return. The cycle comes back to Aries the infant and begins again.**

Thing is, babies can be tiny tyrants with no concept of anyone else but themselves. Give infants milk and they figure that it was their desire for the milk that somehow brought that about, not any effort on your part. Aries adults are the same way. Like their fellow fire signs Leo and Sag, they require your full attention, and their sense of entitlement can be in the upper ranges of ridiculous. In fact, your total service is their expectation. Aries comedian Martin Lawrence performed a bit in his last stand-up movie about collapsing and being semiparalyzed and then falling in love with his nurse because she would literally wipe his ass while bedridden. Real Aries moment.

Take this one Aries cat we know. Cat is seeing this chick, right? Driving her SUV, using her cell phone, etc. Now one day an unfamiliar number comes up on her phone. So, being an Aries, he confronts her about it. When her answer is unsatisfactory, he tosses *her* phone out of the window of *her* car and then refuses to pick *her* up from work in *her* car. Why she puts up with the madness might have something to do with (1) her long-suffering Capricorn nature (see page 103) or (2) the fact that he's slinging that thing in the bedroom somethin' awful. But we're getting ahead of ourselves.

But to be fair, this is just one side of the Aries dialectic. They can also be gifted, charming, and inspiring. Even Suge, for all his gangsta tactics, had enormous ambition and a real-deal work ethic. And when you set aside all the rumors of violent antics, you'll recognize he was

HEAD SUPREME:

PART OF WHAT MAKES

ARIES LIKE DIVA DIANA

ROSS STAND OUT FROM

THE CROWD IS THEIR

BIG HEADS.

a pioneering figure in addressing some of the historical inequities accepted as common practice in an industry full of gangsters. Groundbreakers like Billie Holiday, Marvin Gaye, Francis Ford Coppola, Aretha Franklin, Paul Robeson, Herbie Hancock, and Colin Powell rank among Aries folk who have inspired millions to follow in their footsteps. It makes sense too that Afrika Bambaataa, one of the founding fathers of hip-hop, is Aries. Remember the Daisy Age? Yup, Posdnous of De La Soul had all of us flip our wardrobe for a minute. Don't front.

Free of guile, Aries are usually direct and full of force. Courage comes naturally. And because they are naturally optimistic and overconfident, good things happen for them. Consequently, they get what they want more often than not.

Physically, they're all head. Real-life bobbleheads. It might seem funny, but it's one of the secrets of their charisma. They're easy to spot. Look real close at the Aries stars: Big-head Billy Dee Williams. Eddie Murphy. Martin Lawrence. Stephanie Mills. Star Jones.

When it comes down to it, for the Aries their dick do the talkin'. Metaphorically speaking, of course—dick as in the mannish ego, the pushy, demanding, lemme-in aspect of the human psyche. And if an Aries is female, then her inner dick do the talkin'. That is not always a bad thing, mind you. Like in the bedroom, for example. Rams got that fire under the sheets. High libido. A real appetite and not ashamed to say so. Quite capable of giving you the business, sexually speaking. Both the men and the women get right down to it, but can be playful about the whole thing too. Still, it's a high-impact situation, if you get our meaning.

Interestingly, while the Aries female can, when necessary, get mannish on dat ass, the undercurrent of male energy flowing just below the surface usually doesn't take away from her real-deal sexiness. If anything, it increases it. First, she's open and expressive. Second, she approaches sex with a conqueror's mentality. Kim Cattrall's character, Samantha, on *Sex in the City* is a thoroughly Aries persona. Again, Da Brat is a good example of Aries sexiness. She released three albums before a stylist could persuade her to dress like a woman, and when she finally did, gottdamn! Homegirl was on fire.

If you take a survey of the certified divas from the past few eras, more than likely they're fire signs, and of those more than a few are Aries: Billie Holiday, Diana Ross, Chaka Khan, Aretha Franklin, Sarah Vaughan, Mariah Carey, Jill Scott, and the list goes on. It might be the plaintive wail of a child that we hear in their voices, but it's also that Aries sexual charisma that draws us to them.

But be warned: their game is tight and is to get your ass open so you give them exactly what they

ALWAYS BE YOUR BABY:
MANY ARIES (LIKE MARIAH
CAREY) TEND TO LIVE IN
A SUSPENDED CHILDHOOD.

want. Sex is a weapon, one used with skill and without qualm. And if you are fortunate enough to bed an Aries woman, we suggest you represent like you in Congress. Really twist that back out. Get at the stone or Viagra or whatever is going to maintain your energy level, 'cause if you don't, chick will be lookin' at the front door. If you cannot satisfy her she will let you know. It could get ugly. Unless she loves you; things change if Aries catch feelins. When in love Aries, both men and women, are intensely loyal.

Okay, maybe just the women.

All this violence and sexuality and pioneering and initiative are brought about because Aries is whatchu might call up-tempo. Sometimes too up-tempo. Leaping before they look is regular business for Aries types. Aries are motivated by impulse and, like their fire-sign sistren and brethren (Leo and Sagittarius), are the type to stay in fifth gear all the time. No brakes. No reverse.

It's all in how they manage their fire. The fire can be warm and life-giving, or it can rage out of control and burn everything and everyone in sight. As the first of the fire signs, Aries is particularly susceptible to the element's extremes. If not careful, these personality types are prone to "flaming out": Marvin Gaye, Billie Holiday, Chaka Khan, Martin Lawrence, Robert Downey, Jr., all struggled to contain their fire-born demeanors. In Q-Tip's case, instead of his personality, it was his massive record collection that literally went up in flames.

All in all, Aries plays the warrior: confronting challenges without hesitation, bringing that drama to whoever wants it. Impatient, somewhat gruff, and magnetic, Aries keeps it hot wherever and however. Always in danger of going too far and doing too much. But when they're on point and their selfishness is placed in check, Aries are charismatic boundary breakers, soldiers to a higher cause, full of valor. They got the nerve to affect real change in their arena, whatever it may be.

THE INFAMOUS

Kareem Abdul-Jabbar, Maya Angelou, Pearl Bailey, Afrika
Bambaataa, Rick Barry, Warren Beatty, David Blaine, Elton
Brand, Marlon Brando, Jennifer Capriati, Mariah Carey, Liz
Claiborne, Eric Clapton, Jimmy Cliff, Francis Ford Coppola,
Da Brat, Claire Danes, Shannen Doherty, Tony Dorsett, Buster
Douglas, Robert Downey, Jr., Kenneth "Babyface" Edmonds,
Carmen Electra, Aretha Franklin, Walt Frazier, Andy Garcia,
Marvin Gaye, Al Green, Clara McBride Hale (Hale House founder),
Herbie Hancock, Billie Holiday, Harry Houdini, Kate Hudson, Elton
John, Norah Jones, Star Jones, Ashley Judd, Chaka Khan, Marion
"Suge" Knight, Lucy Lawless, Martin Lawrence, Ananda Lewis,
Bob Mackie, John Madden, Moses Malone, Stephanie Mills,
Moses, Eddie Murphy, John Oates, Sarah Jessica Parker, Teddy
Pendergrass, Popeye, Colin Powell, DJ Premier, Tito Puente,
Keisha Knight Pulliam, Q-Tip, Redman, Paul Robeson, Diana
Ross, Annabella Sciorra, Jill Scott, Steven Seagal, William
Shatner, Naomi Sims, Paul Sorvino, Gloria Steinem, Julia Stiles,
John Stockton, Sheryl Swoopes, Quentin Tarantino, Peter Tosh,
Luther Vandross, Vincent van Gogh, Sarah Vaughan, Christopher
Walken, Booker T. Washington, Muddy Waters, Billy Dee Williams,
Pharrell Williams

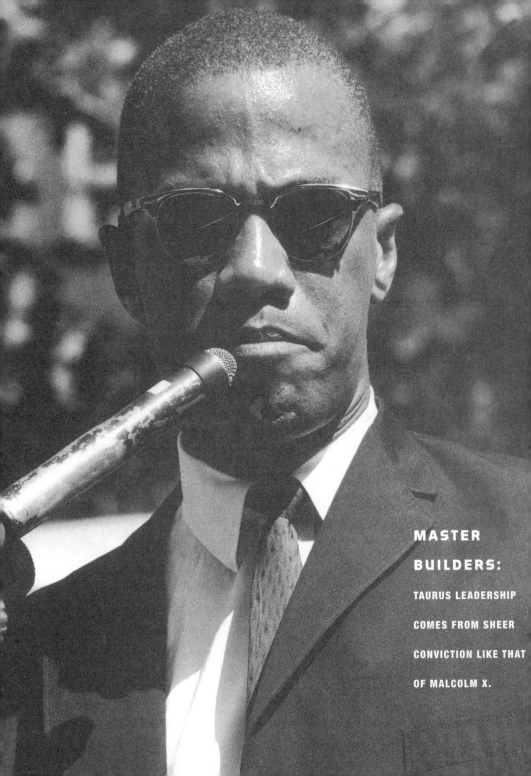

**MASTER
BUILDERS:**

TAURUS LEADERSHIP
COMES FROM SHEER
CONVICTION LIKE THAT
OF MALCOLM X.

TAURUS 04.20–05.20

'BOUT IT, 'BOUT IT

THE RUNDOWN

feminine, *fixed, earth*

Motto *I have*

Sound bite *"Greed is good"* (Gordon Gekko in Wall Street)

Ruling planet *Venus*

Color *pale blue*

Rock *emerald*

Physical *neck and throat*

Icon *Wall Street bull*

Genius *Malcolm X*

Beverage *Courvoisier*

Guilty pleasure *coppin' twenty-four-inch rims*

Accessory *money counter*

Ride *BMW X3*

Find them *at the dealership*

Visual *Scarface*

Moment *Master P wrapping his helicopter in Gucci logos*

THE RUNDOWN

Street occupation/grind *drug lord*

Mix tape *Too $hort, "Gettin' It"; Master P, "Is There a Heaven 4 a Gangsta?," "'Bout It, 'Bout It"; Busta Rhymes, "Put Your Hands Where My Eyes Could See"; Ghostface Killah, "Cherchez LaGhost"; Janet Jackson, "Control," "Pleasure Principle"; Stevie Wonder, "Do I Do"; Junior M.A.F.I.A., "Get Money"; EPMD, "Strictly Business"; Ralph Tresvant, "Sensitivity"*

Best-case scenario *Stevie Wonder*

Worst-case scenario *Adolf Hitler*

Spot *St. Louis, ancient Egypt*

Erogenous zone *bank vault*

Vice *greed*

Natural talent *makin' money*

Compatibilities *Libra, Scorpio, Capricorn*

GHETTO INDEX

Gangstability	9	████████████
Booty quotient	7	█████████
Bling quotient	8	██████████
Drama quotient	2	███
Don status	7	█████████
Trick status	5	███████
Game quotient	6	████████
Shiest quotient	4	█████
Freak quotient	9	████████████

Money, power, sex. That's what's up for the majority of Taureans. To borrow a phrase from someone, Taurus folk are sexually attracted to money. It's why Taurean pimpdaddy and world-renowned freak Too $hort spells his name with the dollar sign. The Taurean gets off from getting it. It's the joy of acquisition, really, and a deep-seated appreciation for the sensual things in life. Money, cars, clothes, houses, furniture, good food, fine wine, and wet sex. There's never enough.

A Taurus prostitute, rationalizing her occupation, said exactly what motivated her in plain

"WHO PUT THIS THING TOGEVER?": *SCARFACE*'S TRAGIC HERO, TONY MONTANA, WAS A COMPLEX COMBINATION OF TAUREAN STUBBORNNESS AND GREED.

15

TAURUS

language: "Look, all this I'm doin' right now, all this hustlin', it's all about havin' thangs." Houses, loved ones, and possessions are more than important to Tauruses; they're crucial. The fear of losing it once it's had runs hella deep.

They live by the pleasure principle. Bling is regular business. Sensual types, they appreciate the finer things in life and will indulge themselves once work is done. Blame it on Venus, their ruling planet. In the same way Mars makes Aries warlike and hype, Venus makes Taurus comfort-loving and hungry. The love planet also blesses Taureans with grace. There is an artistic quality to the way they go about everything they do. Taurus legend Duke Ellington, one of the great American composers, was as monumental a figure for his immaculate style and panache as he was for his legendary compositions and band. On the more garish side of things, Liberace, the original bling king, made lavish luxury his trademark. Cat had sapphires bigger than ice cubes. Taureans are obsessed with acquiring the best available. This lust for the finer things in life is ultimately what gives them their infamous determination.

Although not incredibly ambitious initially, when Taureans are motivated they are excellent workers. Their energy is slow-moving but steady and consistent. Dependable and hardworking, like fellow earth signs Capricorn and Virgo, they make it happen. 'Bout it. Sturdy, hardworkin' folk. Steady, slow-burning. But if the work ethic is not instilled in them early, Taureans can also be the laziest maufuckers in the world.

When they're roused to anger, it gets real ugly. Their normally sweet disposition turns real nasty. When Taurus actor Ving Rhames, in his role as a raped drug dealer in *Pulp Fiction,* announces he's going to "get medieval on your ass" to his rapists, it's the Taurus in him talking. A Taurean defeat is a rare thing.

Tauruses are blessed with enormous strength both physically and psychologically. They take on the traits of the bull. Physically, they tend to have broad shoulders and beautiful necks. Many have the gorgeous limpid eyes and long lashes of a bovine, and an overall thickness that comes from their lavish eating habits. World Wrestling Entertainment star The Rock, whose muscular arms are tatted with the insignia of the bull, exemplifies the highly evolved Taurus physical standard. Janet Jackson, who has had a thirty-year war with her Taurus thickness, makes some of her ghetto fans wish she would just stop playing and keep the onion she had in the "Pleasure Principle" video. Get off that white-girl shit. But we digress. Tauruses, also like their bovine symbol, have a lazy, slow-moving way about them, and their vision can be tunnel. For the most part, they deal with the here and now. They go for what they know. All the high-falutin' theoretical talk goes in one ear and out the other. Not interested. The earth sign in them says it's all about what's going to put that bird in my hand. Fuck the two in the bush.

Like the opposite sign, Scorpio, Taurus has a natural inclination for sex, money, and power. Taureans have strength of purpose, patience, and real-deal conviction. They can also be blind, obstinate, and caught up in materialism. But when that's balanced with a sense of a greater mission, they make excellent leaders and foundation builders. They have the arrogance, determination, and steadfastness to start far-reaching movements. James Brown, the undisputed Godfather of Soul, laid the foundation for most popular music today. Master P started building a five-hundred-million-dollar fortune from the trunk of his car. At the height of his fame, he could have easily run for political office and won. He called his fans soldiers, and they followed his lead. Many fans tatted his No Limit tank logo on their bodies. (Hmmm. Wonder how they feel about them tattoos now?) Jay-Z's business partner, Damon Dash, turned Roc-A-Fella and Rocawear into household names. Taurus Malcolm X, one of the handful of universally acknowledged black American leaders, transformed millions of minds through the sheer force of his will and charisma. Tauruses are more charismatic than a maufucka. They got a magnetic way about them. But don't think their ability to move the crowd hasn't proved to be disastrous as well: in the seventies, Taurus Jim Jones convinced almost a thousand of his followers to commit mass suicide in Guyana. Taurus madman Adolf Hitler led Germany and then all of Europe into World War II, resulting in millions of deaths.

Taureans have large appetites, sexually speaking. The men are what Jamaicans call stamina daddies (fe de gal pickiney, as they'd say in Jamaican patois). They can go on and on. The women can deep-throat with the best of them. Their necks are generally incredibly sensitive, serving as erogenous zones. Wanna get a Taurus open? Do some ol' *9½ Weeks*–type shit: Blindfold them and feed them all manner of food. Cherries, whipped cream, honey. Rub it awll ohvah their body. Get at the powder, the feathers, some rubber, some leather. Anything that exploits the senses. That's if they don't do it to you first—but Taurus will be willing. Taken to the extreme, Taurus might have a thing for must, dirt, even coprophilia. (If you never heard of coprophilia, we refer you to the intro skit to "Nasty Boy" on Biggie's *Life After Death* and won't say much more.) Bring it like that and the freak in Taurus don't stop, won't stop. Just ask renowned freak Too $hort. He'll tell you.

Ironically, it's only in these sorts of pleasures that Taureans let go of their deeply conservative nature. These are some stick-to-the-script, no deviation, no improvisation, my-mother-did-it-this-way-and-that-is-the-way-it's-going-to-stay type folk. This not only ensures their comfort, it is their way of maintaining a certain amount of control. Once a bull stops, there is no moving it. The life lesson for Taureans is learning to let go. They can be so afraid of change that they become stuck and boring—in need of an enema. Typical of earth signs, they find security in their possessions, and once comfortable, they rarely want to risk losing anything. To call them risk-averse is understating it.

Want to fuck with a Taurus? Try to force them to change. Or intervene with their money machine. All that Venus shit goes out the window. There are some trust issues here, for real. But if a Taurus is kept relatively loose, he or she is a natural-born winner with the drive, talent, and power to make it happen. Money ain't a thing.

THE INFAMOUS

Andre Agassi, Jessica Alba, Nick Ashford, Richard Avedon, Pierce Brosnan, James Brown, Buddha, Busta Rhymes, Kelly Clarkson, George Clooney, Penélope Cruz, Damon Dash, Craig David, Duke Ellington, Giancarlo Esposito, Linda Evangelista, Kim Fields, Ella Fitzgerald, Jean Paul Gaultier, Ghostface Killah, Lorraine Hansberry, Keith Haring, Hill Harper, Adolf Hitler, Saddam Hussein, Enrique Iglesias, Janet Jackson, Reggie Jackson, Judith Jamison, Grace Jones, Jim Jones, Harvey Keitel, Coretta Scott King, Christian Lacroix, Jay Leno, Sugar Ray Leonard, Jet Li, Liberace, Sonny Liston, Traci Lords, Joe Louis, Niccolò Machiavelli, Lee Majors, Malcolm X, Master P, Jack Nicholson, Al Pacino, Ma Rainey, Ving Rhames, Sugar Ray Robinson, The Rock, Jimmy Ruffin, William Shakespeare, Kimora Lee Simmons, Tammi Terrell, Isiah Thomas, Uma Thurman, Too $hort, Ralph Tresvant, Terrie Williams, August Wilson, Stevie Wonder, Renée Zellweger

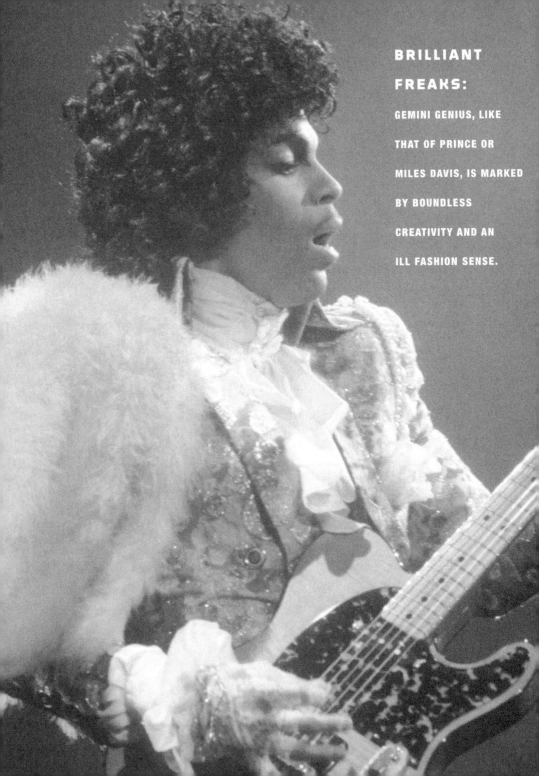

BRILLIANT FREAKS: GEMINI GENIUS, LIKE THAT OF PRINCE OR MILES DAVIS, IS MARKED BY BOUNDLESS CREATIVITY AND AN ILL FASHION SENSE.

GEMINI 05.21–06.20

MIND GAMES

THE RUNDOWN

masculine, *mutable, air*

Motto *I think*

Sound bite *"You gonna let him play you like that?"*

Ruling planet *Mercury*

Color *yellow*

Rock *agate*

Physical *arms, lungs*

Icon *Wonder Twins*

Genius *Miles Davis*

Beverage *Incredible Hulk*

Guilty pleasure *runnin' they mouth*

Accessory *two-way pagers*

Ride *Mini Cooper*

Find them *shooting dice*

Visual Fight Club, *Dre 3000's* "Hey Ya!"

THE RUNDOWN

Moment *Prince changing his name to an unpronounceable symbol*

Street occupation/grind *numbers runner, the negotiator*

Mix tape *2Pac and the Notorious B.I.G., "Running"; Prince, "Sign 'O' the Times"; Miles Davis, Bitches Brew; Spragga Benz, "We Nuh Like"; Bounty Killer, "Sufferer"; OutKast, "Elevators"; Heavy D & the Boyz, "We Got Our Own Thang"; Lenny Kravitz, "Fly Away"; Carl Thomas and Faith Evans, "Emotional"*

Best-case scenario *Venus Williams*

Worst-case scenario *La Toya Jackson*

Spot *back-room gambling spot*

Erogenous zone *backseat of the jeep*

Vice *talk too fuckin' much*

Natural talent *instigatin', storytelling*

Compatibilities *Virgo, Libra, Sagittarius*

GHETTO INDEX

Gangstability	7	
Booty quotient	6	
Bling quotient	4	
Drama quotient	8	
Don status	5	
Trick status	3	
Game quotient	9	
Shiest quotient	10	
Freak quotient	6	

THE BASICS

Wanna know what's hot in the streets? Wanna know who's runnin' shit, who just got shot, what shoes to cop? Check your local Gemini. These folk are information brokers. They catalog the trends, the beefs, the affairs, the who's who and the what's what. But it's not a dispassionate, unbiased, detached approach to the news. Geminis get involved, choose sides, pop mad shit, and be instigating. Typical Gemini opening line: "I don't know if you want to know this, but . . ." Instigators par excellence. No conscience. No, let us amend that: selective conscience. They stay in that middleman position, standing between this and that. Can get quite grimy if they have the mind to. These are high-level intellects with quick wits and platinum tongues.

They speak in codes. Geminis revel in sharing the latest slang. They are masters and mistresses of language, particularly the ever-morphing slanguage of the day. Flutter-tongued niggas, they talk too damn quick and too damn much. Got a lot of special effects in their speech. Many comedians among these folk. Communicating in secret code serves their particular talents well. It is an intellectual exercise that demands quick thinking—from you, that is. Like its next-door neighbor on the zodiac, Cancer, Gemini has a pretty good memory and an eye for detail. Any new form of code or language is seen as a challenge to the Gemini mentality, one they accept with relish.

But to be real, stimulus of any sort is within Gemini jurisdiction. Wing chung, jazz music, Yoruba gods, dog training, TEC-9s, game shows, sports, Buddhism, what have you, all are as likely as the next to be of interest to the Gemini. Most interesting to Geminis? Geminis. Narcissism runs in the blood. Still, Geminis, like the other air signs, Libra and Aquarius, take pride in knowing. The problem with Gemini's interest, and anyone who has dated a Gemini can attest to this, is that it is like a sale: for a limited time only! Whatever energy they throw at you is going to be thrown elsewhere very, very soon. They feed on novelty, and unless you got a bottomless bag of tricks in your repertoire, Gemini is on to the next thing. Believe that. Don't get us wrong; Gemini could be your friend forever. But do not expect consistent attention. Nor should you expect fidelity. Give that pipe dream up riiiiight now. Geminis are a lot of things; monogamous is not really one of them. There are a few exceptions, but there are too many factors going on in the Gemini psyche to really, really expect them to be one-on-one.

Sexually speaking, Geminis are big talkers. Can chat you up like no other while intimate. Probably the best phone sex you'll ever experience. Again, they talk mad shit: whether or not they can back it up half the time is an open question. But Geminis are adventurous and willing to try anything new and intriguing. Their tongue prowess is something to take note of, if you get our meaning. But don't get too open too quickly. Better you prepare for the Big Switch, 'cause it's coming. It's most definitely coming. The Big Switch comes when the other twin, the other personality, takes over the body. Call it fickleness, call it change of mind, but Geminis, like fellow air sign Aquarius, have no concern for yesterday. Or even a few minutes ago. Tomorrow is far more interesting. Geminis keep it moving, emotionally and otherwise.

Another thing one has to realize when fucking with a Gemini on any level: they can drag your ass into some real bullshit. First of all, they got mouth game for days. Rationalization kings and queens. Can convince you that on this particular hour of this particular day black

FILLIN' THEM WITH OCTANE: RULED BY THE PLANET OF COMMUNICATION, GEMINIS LIKE BIGGIE ARE GIFTED WITH THE PLATINUM TONGUE.

just so happens to be white, and *right* is the new word for *wrong.* And, for them, it truly is. Take the time on that *Ready to Die* skit when Biggie explained to his partner why it made sense to rob a crowded subway car: "Is you dead broke, motherfucker?"

Geminis are the great communicators, folk who can tell a tale. Think Tupac, Gladys Knight, Jadakiss, Curtis Mayfield, Lauryn Hill, Miles Davis. These are the messengers, a role most Geminis play skillfully no matter their station in life, be it street thug or mail carrier. But being in that role also gives these trickster maufuckers ample opportunity for mischief. They're prone to get caught up in some type of drama.

Fashion is a major Gemini concern. Again, this is a language they aim to master and use to maximum affect. Geminis don't really follow trends; they push the envelope until it breaks, creating the new paradigms. Gemini genius Prince was niggafying Versace in 1986's *Under the Cherry Moon,* back when most were still pronouncing it "Versakee." Larry Blackmon made some tripped-out shit like the cameo de rigueur for black male hair. Lauryn Hill's style served as the muse for a John Galliano collection and many other fashion designers. Lisa "Left Eye" Lopes, Miles Davis, Pam Grier, and Andre from OutKast, like most Geminis, put enormous amounts of energy into their costumes and outfits. More often than not, Geminis are truly beautiful creatures, and most are quite aware of it. Enhancing this aspect and using this to their benefit is the Gemini way. But it's more than clothing for them; it is, again, a message spoken in code.

Visual languages are also a way of challenging your stilted notions of what is real, what's possible and what's not. Geminis by nature push the boundaries and test the waters. Like children, they are testing the limits of their worlds. To a new world they will be your guide, introducing you to the fauna and warning you of the dangers. If you don't mind the occasional mind game or prank, Geminis actually have a lot to teach.

To really understand Gemini behavior, one must realize that for Geminis it is all a game. Whether you are conscious of it or not, it is one Geminis take very seriously. And play to the end. Never will a Gemini break the rules of this unspoken private game. Take Tupac. Once he chose to be a gangsta, he played by the rules as he understood them. He upheld the street codes, even when it meant sacrificing the many opportunities afforded to someone as gifted, intelligent, and charismatic as he was. He was wholly committed to the game, mind, body, and soul. In the end his strict adherence to such a deadly game would cost him his life, but afford him street immortality. Such is the Gemini story. Such is the Gemini contradiction. Gemini is always both a "thing" and its opposite, a yin and its yang, the one and the two all at the same time.

Throughout the world, twins have been thought to be endowed with mystical powers. In some cultures entire disciplines are devoted to balancing the nature of twins. Even after their deaths, twins are fed, spoken to, and given gifts and sacrifices. Hip-hop had its own twin deities. The saga of Biggie and Tupac was not just the story of two talents taken too soon, it was also the story of Gemini itself. Follow us: Biggie and Tupac were Geminis, like one set of twins paired together. Their lives were marked by an eerie yin-yang symmetry. Everything that Biggie was, Tupac wasn't, and vice versa. Big was a massive, charming comedian who was admittedly hard on the eye. Pac was a small, hot-blooded rah-rah type with butterfly eyelashes and a death wish. They came to define the East Coast/West Coast conflict, but in death they were joined as icons of national ghetto unity. For the individual Gemini, that East Coast/West Coast conflict is waged inside himself.

This duality, sometimes triplicity, sometimes multiplicity, is what everybody loves and hates about Geminis. At times it is dynamic, fun,

29

and damn near magical. (Geminis sometimes seem to be covered in pixie dust, like they come from never-never land or some shit. Other times they are straight out of the comics.) Then again, the Gemini duplicity is ridiculous, idiotic, and shiesty. They live with their contradictions and expect you to do the same. They use their duality with such ruthlessness it leaves friends, associates, and family simply grinding their molars to nubs, grumbling "these motherfuckers . . ." under their breath. But, truth be told, the multiplicity Geminis must manage within themselves is both blessing and curse. All Geminis struggle with their internal warring. At odds with themselves, they must find a coherent way to synthesize diametrically opposed thoughts/emotions/actions. It's enough to drive a maufucka crazy. And it does. Frequently. Think Left Eye. Miles Davis. Angelina Jolie. Boy George. Todd Bridges. Need we go on? Geminis will never be at peace until they can overcome this conflict and teach their warring twins to sing together. Until then, they

are forced to live in a purgatory of extended adolescent struttin', frettin', full of sound and fury signifying nothing. Or as James Brown put it: talking loud, but ain't sayin' nuthin'.

STAY FLIPPIN' IT: **LAURYN'S TRANSFORMATION FROM POP PRINCESS TO ROOTSY SPIRITUALIST IS NOT ATYPICAL FOR A GEMINI.**

THE INFAMOUS

Paula Abdul, Tim Allen, Andre 3000, Carmelo Anthony, Josephine Baker, Larry Blackmon, Boy George, Todd Bridges, Beau Brummell, Naomi Campbell, Miles Davis, El DeBarge, Johnny Depp, D.M.C., Bob Dylan, Clint Eastwood, Paola Fendi, Morgan Freeman, Marla Gibbs, Rudolph Giuliani, Louis Gossett, Jr., Pam Grier, Che Guevara, Heavy D, Lauryn Hill, Ronald Isley, La Toya Jackson, Jadakiss, Jewel, Angelina Jolie, Jenny Jones, John F. Kennedy, Jamaica Kincaid, Gladys Knight, Anna Kournikova, Lenny Kravitz, Lisa "Left Eye" Lopes, Curtis Mayfield, Hattie McDaniel, Brian McKnight, Marilyn Monroe, Alanis Morissette, Mike Myers, S. I. Newhouse (billionaire who ran Condé Nast), the Olsen twins, Natalie Portman, Prince, Phylicia Rashad, Glen Rice, Lionel Richie, Salman Rushdie, Tupac Shakur, Mr. T, Carl Thomas, Philip Michael Thomas, Donald Trump, Mark Wahlberg, Christopher "Biggie" Wallace, Keenen Ivory Wayans, Cornel West, Deniece Williams, Venus Williams

TIG OL' BIDDIES:
BREASTS ARE BOTH
SYMBOLS AND ACCESSORIES
FOR CANCER WOMEN LIKE
PAMELA ANDERSON.

BIG MOMMA THANG

THE RUNDOWN

feminine, *cardinal, water*

Motto *I feel*

Sound bite *"Who could love you like I do?"*

Ruling planet *moon*

Color *sea green, platinum*

Rock *pearl*

Physical *breasts*

Icon *Pamela Anderson*

Genius *Giorgio Armani*

Beverage *Alizé*

Guilty pleasure *anonymous sex*

Accessory *breast implants*

Ride *Escalade*

Find them *in the crib*

Visual *Pam Anderson's honeymoon video*

Moment *Diana Ross fondling Lil' Kim's breast at the MTV awards*

THE RUNDOWN

Street occupation/grind *numbers man, club owner*

Mix tape *Lil' Kim, "Big Momma Thang"; Super Cat, "Ghetto Red Hot"; Missy Elliott, "Get Ur Freak On," "Work It"; Evelyn "Champagne" King, "Love Come Down"; Michael Jackson, "Human Nature"; the Intruders, "I'll Always Love My Mama"; 50 Cent, "21 Questions"; Blondie, "Rapture"*

Best-case scenario *Nelson Mandela*

Worst-case scenario *Mike Tyson*

Spot *Milan*

Erogenous zone *shower*

Vice *trickin'*

Natural talent *photographic memory*

Compatibilities *Pisces, Scorpio, Sagittarius*

GHETTO INDEX

Gangstability	4	
Booty quotient	8	
Bling quotient	6	
Drama quotient	5	
Don status	4	
Trick status	10	
Game quotient	7	
Shiest quotient	2	
Freak quotient	9	

Blame the hormones. Or, better yet, put it on the moon. The moodiness, the emotional shifting, the lunacy, the outlandish shit coming out their mouths are the moon's gifts to her Cancer children. The moon also endows Cancers with a highly sensitive, highly changeable nature. They can be the loveliest, warmest people in the world, and two days later they can put the crab in the phrase "crab-ass nigga." Cancers be tripping sometime. Might get real funny style out of the blue. Their rapid and rampant mood changes could test the patience of Buddha. The comforting thing is that they get funny style on a schedule. If you take notice, their dark side appears at regular intervals. Like the tide, it comes in, it goes out. But more than the mood changes, what no one on God's green earth is prepared for is the profusion of tears. Cancers are some cryin'-ass maufuckas. Big-ass crybabies. Tears fall at the slightest provocation! Li'l Momo graduating kindergarten? Tears. Jackie got diagnosed with fibroids? Tears. Guest on Maury lost two hundred pounds? Grab the kleenex. Cutting onions in the kitchen? Well . . . we guess that's all right. But you see what we're sayin'.

Cancers' moods are more often than not reflective of their home situations. For Cancers, if the home front is all right then it's all good. If not, there is no consoling them and no escape from their foul temperaments and fucked-up attitudes. Family is paramount. Moms is the be-all end-all. The Cancer/Ma-dukes connection wavers around WHOA. We once knew a Cancer cat who stayed living in his momma's crib till he was well into his forties. Shit, some *never* leave. While an Aquarius or Aries child might dash into the street without warning, Cancer children are never too far from momma.

Prone to worry, these folk stay on high alert. The glass is definitely half empty and cracked too, if you ask them. Many Cancers have the Charlie Brown syndrome: they stay walking around dragging rain clouds behind them and wondering why they keep getting wet. They never suspect that all their self-pity is prolonging (if not straight-out creating) their suffering. Trusting that everything will be all right is not one of Cancers' strong suits. Overcoming their negative outlook is their greatest challenge.

Consider yourself under surveillance if you live with one. Super-sensitive, these maufuckas peep everything and keep a running tab. Bet you the Cancers are fully up-to-date on the latest turn in cousin Bebe's rocky marriage. That old lady downstairs always glancing out her window on unofficial neighborhood watch? Cancer. That homemaker boohooing over Ricki Lake? Cancer. They are the neighborhood histori-ans, a.k.a. gossipmongers. Cancers be some whispering maufuckas.

Helping all this speculation and cataloging of human events is the fact that Cancerians have elephant memories. They can remem-ber that time when you two were watching *Diff'rent Strokes* together and you spilled the Kool-Aid on the carpet. They remember every slight and hold grudges to the grave. To the grave! And while Cancer is not the most gangsta of signs in the zodiac (that honor goes to the Sag-Scorpio corner of the wheel, followed closely by Aries-Taurus), they do have their weapons. They bind emotion to every incident. Cancer's gangsta manifests three years later when they bring up the time you forgot their birthday and left them waitin' in the rain. And you knew they were fighting a cold at the time, you motherfucker you. Yeah, for the Cancerian it's whatever's necessary to inflict maximum guilt. They take aim with jagged emotional knives, making you suffer as they suffer.

Cancers do everything in a kinda indirect fashion. Like their symbol, the crab, they move sideways. They make secret plans and harbor deep resentments. They don't speak directly. They give hints until that moment their patience wears out and they let you know exactly how they feel with a few choice words. They won't protest a situation; they'd rather manage it. To get a message to you, they might mention something in passing to your girlfriend. In war and conflict, Cancer's inner Machiavelli arises. Cancerians have a calculating way about them, and such a deep understanding of human behavior that prediction and foresight are second nature. But after constructing the perfect plan for victory, a Cancerian might throw it all away on a whim. Cancers are masters at manipulation but slaves to emotion. And they can be emotionally manipulative. Believe that.

Physically, they are ruled by the breast, so breasts are central to Cancer symbolism. As symbols of both sexuality and motherhood, breasteses sum up the two major poles of Cancerian inner life. The Cancer appeal is generally titticentric. More often than not, tig ol' biddies come with the package. Be they natural (Missy Elliott, Lisa Nicole Carson) or saline (Pam Anderson, Lil' Kim), the breasts function as accessories. Even Cancer men like Mike Tyson and Vin Diesel sport sizable man-titties. It's why grown-ass Cancer men can't move out their momma crib: metaphorically, they're still being breast-fed.

In many ways, Cancer men are women in male bodies. Cancers like George Michael, Derek Jeter, and Carl Lewis, among others, come off as slightly "fey" (read: feminine) Not that there are not tough-guy Cancers (Sylvester Stallone, Richard Roundtree, Michael Vick), but usually Cancer men are neat, immaculately dressed, stay close to home, and will always love they mommas more than any other sun

sign. Even thug god Mike Tyson, once the undisputed heavyweight champion of the world, speaks with a high-pitched lisping coyness better suited for a shy young girl. In a parallel to the kind of sexual inversion that happens with females in extra-masculine signs (Aries, Sagittarius), male Cancers suffer from the very femaleness of their zodiac sign. Even more than Libra and Pisces males, who must manage a lot of feminine energy as well, Cancer men live in the turbulent emotional depths usually reserved for women. In the case of Cancerian R&B crooner Joe, this emotionalism gives him a certain charisma, a kinda empathetic advantage in reaching his mostly female audience. Both Richard Roundtree in *Shaft* and Jamaican dancehall legend Supercat flipped the Cancerian charisma into stardom. In the O. J. Simpson trial, we saw both sides of the Cancer man. His Libra lawyer, Johnnie Cochran, depicted O. J. as a typical Cancer: a charming, dedicated father who loved his kids, gave generously to his wife's family, and was falsely accused of a crime he could never commit. Prosecutors presented him as a volatile ex-jock who beat his wife, then murdered her and her friend in a jealous rage. It is particularly possible with Cancer for both to be true. The opposite sign, Capricorn, is equally emotional and the depth of emotion is just as daunting, but Capricorn conceals it under a stiff, rigid exterior of wintry ice. While Cancers build a gruff protective shell, it's a front that doesn't last long. Not long after Tyson threatened to eat Lennox Lewis's kids, Tyson wiped his opponent's brow after their fight and honored Lennox's family! Their feelings show, and in a society where boys ain't supposed to cry, that is some shit to deal with. It's probably why Mike Tyson has had such a rocky time in the glare of celebrity. Simply a case of "the nigga too sensitive." The man who was considered the toughest and meanest in the world could never show his real emotions. Mike was once quoted as saying: "I never had an intellectual problem, I had an emotional problem."

Cancer females are women's women. Feminine, nurturing, caring, sensual—everything this society demands (fairly or unfairly) from

women. They are either (a) natural mothers, or (b) undercover porn stars, or (c) both. Cancerian Pam Anderson is the perfect example. If you came across her honeymoon tape over the Internet you know she's a (c). Sexuality is at the core of their personality. Endowed with an incredible sensuality, many Cancers have those qualities porn stars are made

MAGIC STICK: KIM'S CANCERIAN FEMININITY FORCED FEMALE RAPPERS TO MAKE THEIR STYLE MORE SEXY.

of. Anonymous sex is a lure. They might maintain a secret love life. But despite Pam's sex-bomb persona, she is also a dedicated mother who loves her children. Hip-hop sex kitten Lil' Kim showed her love for her former boyfriend and mentor, the Notorious B.I.G., by mothering and taking care of his entire crew after he died. His *entire crew.* It's the mother thing—she couldn't help it.

Another reason is that Cancer loyalty goes deep. And like the moon, Cancers are reflective. They are excellent mimics and are extremely sensitive to their environments. Lil' Kim was at her Cancerian best as a reflection of the Notorious B.I.G. She was a perfect female counterpart to Biggie's street-level genius, the moon to his sun. When her sun was taken (Biggie was murdered execution-style in Los Angeles), Kim seemed artistically rudderless and without real direction.

Cancer loves the frills. Loves the frills. They enjoy the good life and are willing to go out of their way to indulge in it. They can get caught up in candy and supertrendy baubles. If there is a flaw to their style, it is that they are prone to doing too much. Too much eye shadow, car too flashy, too many sequins, just too much. Lil' Kim, for instance, has been through thousands of different looks.

But along with the mood swings and full-out awareness, both the men and women have an enormous sense of humor. Funny cats. Loony. John Leguizamo is typical of the Cancer talent. His one-man show on Broadway took advantage of his Cancer insights and warped way of looking at things. It is this sense of the ridiculous, this way of not taking themselves too seriously, that is Cancers' saving grace. It is what allows them to overcome pessimism and black clouds and create the success they demand from life: material and emotional stability, regular sex, and a loyal family around them. Give this to Cancer and the moodiness, complaining, and nagging might just disappear. (We emphasize the word *might.*)

THE INFAMOUS

Pamela Anderson, Jean-Bertrand Aristide, Giorgio Armani, Arthur Ashe, Beck, Bill Blass, Charlie Brown, Pierre Cardin, Stokely Carmichael, Diahann Carroll, Lisa Nicole Carson, Bill Cosby, Tom Cruise, Willem Dafoe, the Dalai Lama, Larry David, Oscar de la Renta, Princess Diana, Missy Elliott, John Elway, 50 Cent, Danny Glover, David Alan Grier, Tom Hanks, Deborah "Blondie" Harry, King Henry VIII, Lena Horne, Derek Jeter, Joe, Frida Kahlo, Nicole Kidman, Michelle Kwan, John Leguizamo, Carl Lewis, Lil' Kim, Courtney Love, Magoo, Tobey Maguire, Nelson Mandela, Cheech Marin, Thurgood Marshall, George Michael, Claudette Ortiz, Della Reese, John D. Rockefeller, Richard "Shaft" Roundtree, Barry Sanders, Carlos Santana, Jessica Simpson, O. J. Simpson, Jimmy Smits, Leon Spinks, Sly Stallone, Cree Summer, Supercat, Liv Tyler, Mike Tyson, Jesse Ventura, Michael Vick, Jimmie Walker, Faye Wattleton, Forest Whitaker, Wendy Williams

DIVA LIVE:

LEOS LIKE JENNIFER

LOPEZ LIVE ON THE

ASSUMPTION THAT

THEY SHOULD BE

TREATED LIKE

ROYALTY.

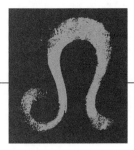

ALL EYES ON ME

THE RUNDOWN

masculine, *fixed, fire*

Motto *I will*

Sound bite *"Do you know who I am?"* (Leo turned away at a club)

Ruling planet *sun*

Color *gold, orange*

Rock *ruby*

Physical *heart*

Icon *Lion of Judah*

Genius *Madonna*

Beverage *Crown Royal*

Guilty pleasure *exhibitionism*

Accessory *crown, tiara*

Ride *Hummer H2*

Find them *on stage*

Visual The Lion King

Moment *Jennifer Lopez arrives with P. Diddy in the green Versace dress*

THE RUNDOWN

Street occupation/grind *gang leader*

Mix tape *Public Enemy, "Rebel Without a Pause"; Kurtis Blow, "If I Ruled the World"; The Wiz soundtrack, "(I'm a) Mean Ole Lion"; Boogie Down Productions, "Criminal Minded"; Jennifer Lopez, "Jenny from the Block"; Madonna, "Express Yourself"; Kool Moe Dee, "How Ya Like Me Now"; Whitney Houston, "I Will Always Love You"*

Best-case scenario *Haile Selassie*

Worst-case scenario *Mussolini*

Spot *Hollywood*

Erogenous Zone *under the spotlight*

Vice *arrogance*

Natural talent *grandstandin'*

Compatibilities *Capricorn, Scorpio, and other Leos*

GHETTO INDEX

Gangstability	6	
Booty quotient	8	
Bling quotient	9	
Drama quotient	6	
Don status	7	
Trick status	7	
Game quotient	8	
Shiest quotient	5	
Freak quotient	6	

Voted Most Likely to Have a Godlike Complex. Leos be feeling them-selves and operate under the assumption that you should too. Granted they are charismatic and funny and got a way about them, but damn, nigga! Folk be straight ODin' on themselves. They blur the line be-tween legitimate self-confidence and outright arrogance. What gets them over, though, is that in spite all of the eye-rolling and playa-hating they arouse, these catlike folk intrigue, entertain, enrage, or inspire just about everybody they come into contact with. No matter what your feelings about these folk, it's a safe bet you ain't bored.

As for the Leos, they could give a fuck what you think. They are in it strictly for the immediate gratification: if you got it for them, great. If you don't, they're off to find someone who does. A Leo is the kind to get his dick sucked in the Oval Office.

PLAYER PRESIDENT: CLINTON DEFINES LEO COOL. INTELLIGENT, CHARMING, AND SHAMELESS, THEY'LL GAME THE PANTIES OFF YOU.

45

LEO

Whut? Leo Bill Clinton—the Playa President—was faced with his, like, fifth sex scandal in a row—you know, the one that nearly cost him the presidency. The president's libido was becoming a major national distraction. The Republicans were smelling blood, evidence was mounting, and he had to give the State of the Union. It was a textbook Leo performance. With the entire nation watching to see how he would respond to the tape recordings, the perjury charges, the calls for his impeachment, the cum stains on homegirl's dress, he gave a bang-up State of the Union address (summary: shit is great) without blinking an eye and did the George Jefferson walk out the United States Capitol like it was business as usual. You knew that he knew that you knew that he was lying about that girl. That didn't matter. He'd just bite his lip and ask if you believed him or your lying eyes. But what rankled his enemies most was that underneath all of Clinton's legalese and half-hearted apologies was the attitude and voice of a nigga grabbing his dick: "What? I'm that motherfucker. I smoke weed. And? Oh, Monica? The chick wanted some. I obliged. The fuck. . . ." On some straight Tony Soprano shit.

Okay, we're putting words in his mouth, but Leos be on it like that. These are the most getting-away-with-murder folk on the planet. How? Game. Pure and simple. Leo game contains the following ingredients: one part magnetism, three parts natural luck, two parts hair, two parts flash, and five parts unrelenting will. Oh, and ten parts pure, uncut audacity. In fact, audacity is not enough to describe the kind of chutzpah demonstrated by these loud, in-your-face, tryin'a-order-you-around maufuckas. Leos speak fluent imperative. The most notorious divas were born under the sign of Leo: J.Lo. Madonna. Iman. Whitney. Highly specific demands, violent temper tantrums, and ruthless dismissals are all part of the Lionesses' repertoire.

Physically, Leos actually look feline. They usually have wide, high cheekbones and large and expressive or slightly almond-shaped cat-like eyes. They are either tall with graceful bodies in that pre-Bobby Whitney Houston vein, or slightly shorter with plenty of heft to them like J.Lo. Both male and female can be highly attractive. Hair is big with the lionfolk. They are infamous for their manes: George Clinton, Kelis, Madonna, Lucille Ball, Coolio, all use hair as a major accessory. If Leos are not sporting a huge, sometimes reddish, attention-grabbing mane, they are as likely to fly to the other extreme and rock a baldy like Leo actor Wesley Snipes. Dreadlocks, made popular by reggae and hip-hop, is one of the most identifiable Leonine hairstyles there is. But we'll come back to the dread-Leo connection later.

The Leo craves attention like it's nicotine. The spotlight must be shining squarely on they ass for a Leo to feel like there's order to the universe. Likely to have fits if not given their four squares of attention a day—the male Leo in particular. Leo legend and basketball giant Wilt Chamberlain once boasted that he bedded thousands of women. No need to remind anyone of Bill Clinton's exploits, but, needless to say, he was on some real Leo shit. But the male Leo's need for female attention is grandeur. When sexually involved with a Leo, understand that, more often than not, it is all about them. Leo sex talk be somethin' like: I knew you wanted to fuck me, or tell me I'm the one, or tell me I'm fucking the shit out of you, or tell me you love it. Something to that effect. Don't get it twisted. In relationships, unless you are an equally powerful and forceful sign (Taurus, Scorpio, Aquarius) it's their way or the highway. In the movie that is constantly playing in their head, they are always getting ready for their close-up. You? You got a choice: you can be best supporting actor, or you're making a cameo appearance. Take your pick.

SHOWTIME: FLASH IS ALWAYS PART OF THE LEO PACKAGE. LEO MAGIC JOHNSON PLAYED EYE-PLEASING BASKETBALL.

To be fair, though, the attention thing is a general fire-sign situation. The other two fire signs—Aries and Sagittarius—suffer from the same deep-seated need. Like fire itself, they all need to be tended to, fueled, and stoked. Without such attention, fire goes out. This is particularly true with Leo. The good thing, though, is that Leos burn warm and bright. They usually make all the attention you must pay them worth it. They put on a hellified show. Leo and All-Star NFL cornerback Deion Sanders, who was known for his incredible speed and his camera-ready style of play, arrived on his college campus with his flash fully intact. As a freshman on his first day of college he drove up in a shiny new car with vanity plates that read PRIME TIME, a nickname that would stick. Another example of Leo showmanship at the highest level is legend Magic Johnson. Magic held court in the glamour capital of the world for nearly a decade, where he led the Los Angeles Lakers to four NBA titles. His flamboyant brand of offense, with its alley-oop plays and no-look passes, was dubbed "Showtime." (Do we detect a pattern here?) Los Angeles, which could pass for a Leo city were it not so vapid, crowned him king.

Even after being diagnosed with HIV, a situation that would have devastated most people or sent them into seclusion, Magic still commanded the spotlight. Magic refused to be cowed by the disease or the stigma that usually comes with it. Courage comes naturally to Leos. They face up to any challenge without hesitation. In a few Leos, however, this trait may backfire: they turn into cowardly lions, all bravado but secretly scared to death.

The Leo will, the psychological underpinning that makes them do what they do, is not to be fucked with. Leos know what the fuck they want, and their sense of entitlement is in perfect keeping with those desires. They fully expect to get what they are looking for and will raise holy hell if not satisfied. Folk will go all out. Gettin' down for their crown, as the saying goes. And if not given a crown, Leos rock a crown of their own making. Even if financially broke (which happens, because of Leo's tendency toward extravagance), a Leo will retain an above-it-all attitude.

Leo has an uncanny ability to make the seemingly impossible possible. Leo Fidel Castro has ruled over a Communist nation ninety miles from the United States for the last forty years. Leo Halle Berry has taken Hollywood—a town notoriously unfriendly to black actresses—by storm. Ugly-ass, nondancing Leo Mick Jagger became a sex symbol and a legendary rock star. Look at Latina diva Jennifer Lopez. Truth be told, J.Lo's ass is average ghetto booty (believe us, there's bigger and bouncier), yet it's revered, worshipped, and written about like she invented ass. In the end, she's been able to flip America's fascination with her behind into a record deal, starring movie roles, and a clothing company. Meanwhile, her ass functions as an unofficial trademark. (Booty got maufuckas so hypnotized she got Ben Affleck looking like an accessory in her videos an' shit.) How she do it? Charge it to Leo showmanship. Leos know how to flaunt it.

Charge it to Leo game. They can make mountains out of molehills. How real is Leo game? One word: Madonna. She left Detroit in her teens to pursue a career in music armed with nothing but a mediocre voice and her will to succeed. She became the undisputed queen of pop music, maybe the biggest, most prolific, and most famous female star to ever grace the stage. When she first appeared on the white *Soul Train*—Dick Clark's *American Bandstand*—she was asked what her plans were. She smiled and said, "To rule the world."

She was being quite serious. If Leos decide to do something, there is nothing on this planet that can stop them. Since then, not only did she inspire millions of women and set the standard for an outspoken female star who uses sex, controversy, and style as her weapons, she maintained control over

KING OF KINGS: THE CROWNED KING OF ETHIOPIA, HAILE SELASSIE WALKED ABOUT HIS PALACE WITH HIS PET LIONS. CAN'T REALLY GET MORE LEO.

her career, did what the fuck she wanted, and continues a twenty-year run as one of the biggest forces in pop culture worldwide. Then she decided to have children, get married, and kiss Britney Spears and Christina Aguilera live on national television! And whut? Recognize the game. Leos do whatever they have to to stay in the spotlight.

It is strategy, really. Based on the idea that if you behave like royalty you get treated like royalty. Leos radiate regalness. They mitigate their high expectations and irascible behavior with a good sense of humor and an endearing way. His majesty Haile Selassie, the last king of Ethiopia and the very definition of highly evolved Leo qualities (not only was he king of Ethiopia and called the Lion of Judah, he had pet lions!), came from a noble family and, although not directly in line for the crown at the time, always had a confidence about him. This caught the attention of the elders of the royal court and led to his being given responsibility, and ultimately to his being crowned king.

Rastafari is a Leo religion through and through. The Rastafarian Christ figure, Emperor Haile Selassie, and one of Rastafari's seminal prophets, Marcus Garvey, were both full-blooded August Leos. Rastas are awash in Leo symbolism: identifying with the sun, lions, and royalty, they believe the corruption of this world will be burned away by a spiritual fire. Capleton, reggae star and another major Leo figure in Rasta consciousness, has become known for his fervent cries "Mo fire! Mo fire!" for the eternal fire to burn Babylon down.

Leos' determination, however, to never let you see them sweat devolves into a state of denial. Cats will front to their dying day. When Diane Sawyer confronted Whitney Houston about the rumors and reports that Whitney did drugs, among them crack cocaine, her response was classic Leo frontin'. "First of all," she said with eyebrows arching, "crack is cheap." Not the most self-critical of folks, Leos do their self-questioning privately, if ever. In public, they never admit to being wrong and would rather cling tightly to some extravagant sense of pride than give anyone the satisfaction.

It is this pride that can potentially damage their natural leadership abilities. Funny, articulate, intelligent, and forceful, they are just the type to lead a crew. *(Right up to your face and dis you!)* Like their opposite sign, Aquarius, they also have a thirst and respect for knowledge, which keeps them well-informed and prepared for almost any challenge. Leos KRS-One and Chuck D of Public Enemy ignited the political consciousness of the entire hip-hop generation, changing the course of American culture forever. (KRS's moniker, standing for Knowledge Reigns Supreme, demonstrates the Leo shit thoroughly.)

In spite of their self-aggrandizing behavior, Leos can actually be very generous. Like their ruling body, the sun, they often give of themselves without too much thought. The more evolved a Leo is, the more likely he or she is in touch with the Rasta concept of the I and I. This is the understanding that the difference between our individual selves and the collective self is an illusion. We are one. So, to serve self is to serve all. When we do for others, we do for ourselves. If Leos grasp this reality, they become more than just talented show-offs, they become unstoppable forces for change: true kings and queens walking among us.

THE INFAMOUS

Ben Affleck, Louis Armstrong, Lucille Ball, Antonio Banderas, Angela Bassett, Halle Berry, Michael Bivins, Kurtis Blow, Riddick Bowe, Sandra Bullock, Fidel Castro, Kim Cattrall, Wilt Chamberlain, Coco Chanel, Bill Clinton, George Clinton, Coolio, Chuck D, Robert De Niro, Fred Durst, Patrick Ewing, Fat Joe, Laurence Fishburne, Kadeem Hardison, Isaac Hayes, Anita Hill, Iman, Mick Jagger, Malcolm Jamal-Warner, Magic Johnson, Kelis, Kool Moe Dee, KRS-One, Lisa Kudrow, Eriq La Salle, Matt LeBlanc, Monica Lewinsky, Jennifer Lopez, Madonna, Debi Mazar, Reggie Miller, Wanya Morris, Robin Quivers, Al Roker, Yves Saint Laurent, Deion Sanders, Arnold Schwarzeneg-ger, Haile Selassie, Sir Mix-a-Lot, Wesley Snipes, Kevin Spacey, Martha Stewart, Superman, Michelle Yeoh

GLITTERING
PERFECTION:
VIRGOS, LIKE BEYONCÉ
AND MICHAEL JACKSON
IN HIS HEYDAY, TWINKLE
LIKE THE NIGHT SKY.

VIRGO 08.24–09.22

SUPER-FLY

THE RUNDOWN

feminine, *mutable, earth*

Motto *I analyze*

Sound Bite *"I analyze, drop a jew-el, . . . school a fool well," (Nas)*

Ruling planet *Mercury*

Color *navy blue, gray*

Rock *sapphire*

Physical *stomach*

Icon *Glinda the Good Witch*

Genius *Nas*

Beverage *Grey Goose*

Guilty pleasure *cleaning*

Accessory *Palm Pilot*

Ride *Audi TT*

Find them *at the Donna Karan outlet*

Visual The Wiz, Superfly

Moment *Michael Jackson walking on lighted sidewalk in "Billie Jean" video*

THE RUNDOWN

Street occupation/grind *keepin' the books*

Mix tape *Beyoncé, "Crazy in Love"; Michael Jackson, Off the Wall; Nas, "It Ain't Hard to Tell," "Mastermind"; Big Daddy Kane, "Smooth Operator"; Run-D.M.C., "Perfection"; Afrika Bambaataa, "Looking for the Perfect Beat"; Ludacris, "What's Your Fantasy"*

Best-case scenario *Michael Jackson (presurgery)*

Worst-case scenario *Michael Jackson (post-Bad)*

Spot *Paris, Harlem*

Erogenous zone *fancy restaurant bathroom*

Vice *hypercritical*

Natural talent *organizing thought*

Compatibilities *Gemini, Pisces, Taurus*

GHETTO INDEX

Gangstability	4	
Booty quotient	7	
Bling quotient	6	
Drama quotient	2	
Don status	4	
Trick status	9	
Game quotient	8	
Shiest quotient	5	
Freak quotient	7	

Virgos got issues, man. Issues. So many they need to cancel their subscription. Yeah, everybody's got issues, but sometimes Virgos wear theirs on their sleeves. Some of this can't be helped. Virgos combine high sensitivity with real practicality, making them uniquely intelligent, detail-oriented, and insightful. This combo can also make them finicky, short-sighted, and full of hang-ups. How it plays out depends on whether or not a Virgo finds a constructive way to busy herself. Use up some of that excess mental energy. 'Cause for Virgos things are never, never right. That lint on your sweater may be the straw that broke the camel's back. That subtle scent of chicken grease at your place might be the reason you ain't getting no pussy tonight. Virgos need distraction from their obsessive-compulsive tendencies.

Where and how they work is particularly important. Full of nervous energy, Virgos have to find a way to deal. Something intricate, involved, and demanding, preferably, otherwise the niggling nelly inside of them will take over. If not, then trouble awaits: nervous twitches, mental breakdowns, stomach problems, health issues, and a cynical attitude nobody can stand.

But give them good reason to show real devotion and the Virgo's natural genius makes itself known: steady, consistent workmanship, without too much pomp and circumstance. Underappreciated, their subtle ways and actions are what make major projects succeed. Think about it: if it weren't for the accountants, planners, and IT motherfuck-

PUSHERMAN: VIRGO RON O'NEAL'S UNDERSTATED GLAMOUR MADE *SUPER-FLY* MORE THAN JUST A MOVIE. IN THE 1970S, IT WAS THE BLUEPRINT FOR STYLE.

ers, do you think any corporations would last beyond a month? If it wasn't for the cameramen, stylists, and make-up artists behind the scenes in the movie industry, do you think you would give a fuck about half these so-called celebrities?

The Virgin, in fact, represents the mystery, the ethereal on-high wisdom untouched by mankind. In some ancient traditions Wisdom was called Sophia and was considered the female aspect of God. In Christian traditions that wisdom is embodied by the Virgin Mary, mother of Jesus (See the Virgo-Pisces Axis, page xxiii), who lived such a pristine life she was chosen by God to bear the Christ child. This is what gives Virgos that otherworldly quality, despite the fact that they are practical, realistic folk. They are "touched." Like their opposite sign, Pisces, Virgos spend a lot of time staring into space, concocting plans, and indulging visions.

This dedication to that ultimate vision is what makes them perfectionists. This aspect of the Virgo psyche was portrayed in the ultimate blaxploitation classic, *Superfly.* This flick was steeped in Virgoness. Set in the Virgo city of Harlem, it introduced us to hustler extraordinaire Priest, played by Virgo actor Ron O'Neal. Precise in his planning, conflicted by his own earthbound needs and concerns, always searching for a better way out, Priest articulated in style and substance the Virgo dilemma. Successful in the cocaine game, with all the coke, fly cars, and white women a seventies black man could want, he still wanted something more. Virgos can't decide whether earth or heaven deserves more of their attention. In this they have something in common with their Mercury-ruled brethren, Gemini. Both are divided souls. Perhaps that explains why Gemini soul man Curtis Mayfield could create the perfect soundtrack for the movie: the Mercury connection.

Perfection is a recurring motif when it comes to Virgos. The way they move is graced with a clean, unsullied quality. Sublime. Type fly. Watch Virgo b-ball prodigy Kobe Bryant do his spin move into the paint or listen to Nas on a cut like "It Ain't Hard to Tell" for proof of the Virgo mastery of detail. Nas has a pristine rhyme style. Always striving for absolute perfection, Virgos are gifted with a meticulous eye and a transcendent style to match. They organize themselves and the space around them in a clear and concise manner. No hair is out of place, no move unconsidered. Even a wilder-type Virgo like, say, Atlanta rapper Ludacris demonstrates such rhythmic exactitude on club anthems like "Move Bitch" and "Throw Dem Bows" that he has become a dancefloor favorite.

The downside of the details thing is that Virgos get caught up in the minutiae. While they master the little things, they often miss the big picture. In other words, the Virgo will see that the painting on the wall is tilted and not realize that actually the entire house is on a slant. This is how the Virgo thing can go all wrong.

Perfectionism can even be catastrophic. The September 11 tragedy reflected all the traits of its obsessive-compulsive zodiac sign. This was a Virgo endeavor through and through, a crime of exactitude, executed with meticulous precision on a pristine fall day. It required long planning, exact accounting, an eye for details, and absolute com-

mitment to the task. It was also Virgolike in that it was other-worldly: a spectacle of biblical propor-tion so horrific it led many to read it as a sign from God. Oh,

BLESSING OR CURSE?: **VIRGOS' PERFECTIONISM (LIKE MICHAEL JACKSON'S) CAN TURN INTO STRAIGHT FREAK SHIT IF THEY ARE NOT CAREFUL.**

add insane to the list too, reflecting the Virgo penchant to take things a little too far.

Commitment is heavy business for Virgos. Virgos and Pisces are probably the signs most willing to die for a cause. Or for you. In a relationship, they can give of themselves totally and completely, sometimes losing perspective, sometimes losing themselves. On her album *M!ssundaztood,* Virgo pop princess Pink sings of her tendency to do just that. Issues. A stable, consistent relationship is crucial for a Virgo to feel secure. Their devotion in relationships is total. A woman who waits till her man finishes a bid? Virgo. Duke who waits on his girl hand and foot? Virgo. Like the other two earth signs (see Taurus and Capricorn), a stable home and a stable relationship are the difference between Virgo excellence and Virgo insanity.

And when they go insane? Critical of everybody and everything, they are most critical of themselves. Virgo Michael Jackson, before all the surgery and bizarre behavior, was the apple of the world's eye. Like many Virgos, Michael was a prodigy. As the Jackson 5's baby frontman, he sung and danced with a maturity far beyond his years. His light but precise dance moves made him everybody's favorite video star. (Don't front—you know you had that ugly-ass *Thriller* jacket.) He ultimately achieved megastardom. Had chicks faintin' an' shit at his shows. But biographers document that even with all the accolades, all the fame, Michael was never satisfied. Extremely hard on himself, always fretting about maintaining his stardom, he considered himself a failure if he didn't sell twenty million records each time out. He was constantly tweaking. His obsession manifested itself in, for one, his addiction to plastic surgery. The tragic element of Michael's overdone facial surgery is that the same instinct toward perfection that made him one of the greatest performers ever to

NO HALF STEP-
PIN': **VIRGO
RAPPERS LIKE
KANE, NAS, AND
LUDACRIS ARE
INFAMOUS FOR
THEIR CLEAN-CUT
STYLE AND
PRECISE RHYMES.**

grace the stage is probably the same thing that made him methodi-
cally destroy his appearance.

Under more normal circumstances, Virgos generally keep it kinda
fly. Michael at his best glittered like a starry night sky. Virgo pretty is a
clean, Noxzema pretty. There's an unblemished, virginal quality to it:
think of Virgos Salma Hayek and Mrs. Will Smith, Jada Pinkett. Like

Kobe, Virgos usually have almond-shaped eyes with smooth skin and full lips. Even if Virgo women are on the thick side, it is usually for the good. Sanaa Lathan, Sophia Loren, and Beyoncé Knowles are all good examples of Virgo thickness.

Icons of style. Virgos rule fashion. The fashion in *Superfly* turned black America out for years. If you wasn't tryin'a look like Virgo Ron O'Neal in the seventies, something was wrong with you. Oooh, and in the eighties, Virgo Big Daddy Kane was that nigga. Bruh was clean! Kane's cameo was so right he made roundhead niggas with no business even thinking about any geometric hairstyle whatsoever embarrass themselves for years. For years! Virgo star Pink's perfectly manicured punk image has made even ghetto chicks flip a rock look.

All that is to say Virgos can be sexy when they wanna be. Although they have reputations as prudes, it's less about the lack of sexual appetite than it is the need for verrry specific conditions to get open. Once they're open, though, the secret freak they've been repressing might come springing out. Do the right thing with a Virgo and that quiet librarian camouflage might be put to the side. Like the virginal Scorpio or the cowardly Leo, there are a few Virgos who play against type. Some are wild, sloppy, and undisciplined. Virgo Charlie "Bird" Parker, one of the fathers of bebop, revered for his intricate style on the tenor sax, was also known for being a dirty, out-of-control heroin addict. In his autobiography, Miles Davis remembers being very young and square and sharing a cab with Bird after a gig. Bird was eating greasy fried chicken and having sex with eager young white girls in the backseat next to him. When Bird noticed Miles looking at him all crazy, he told him if he didn't like it he should look the other way.

There are deep contradictions within Virgos. You know, issues. At their most evolved, Virgos sparkle angelic, coming in like Glinda the

Good Witch and shit in *The Wiz,* bringing the word on high to the earthly plane. At their worst, Virgos turn into overcritical repressed freaks. As with Geminis, both sides reside within them; which one takes control depends on what Virgos do with themselves and the energies running through them. Eazy-E, one of the founders of N.W.A, was the definition of a player: rich, famous, and known to throw wild parties and sleep with hundreds of women, all the while rhyming about it on his platinum-selling albums. He was living in a gangsta's paradise. In 1995, he was diagnosed with AIDS. He died a few months later. And so it's like that with Virgo. Perfection or disillusion. Heaven or hell. Take your pick.

THE INFAMOUS

Fiona Apple, Nate Archibald, Ricky Bell, Beyoncé, Big Daddy Kane, Foxy Brown, Kobe Bryant, designer Stephen Burrows, Tim Burton, Nell Carter, Eldridge Cleaver, Sean Connery, David Copperfield, Celia Cruz, Brian De Palma, Cameron Diaz, Eric Dickerson, Eazy-E, James Gandolfini, Macy Gray, Salma Hayek, Pee Wee Herman, Michael Jackson, Tommy Lee Jones, K-Ci, Ricki Lake, Sanaa Lathan, Lisa Ling, Sophia Loren, Ludacris, Rocky Marciano, Branford Marsalis, Freddie Mercury, Moby, Jelly Roll Morton, "Sugar" Shane Mosley, Mickey Mouse, Bill Murray, Nas, Ron O'Neal (*Superfly*), Charlie "Bird" Parker, Rosie Perez, River Phoenix, Pink, Otis Redding, Keanu Reeves, Guy Ritchie, Gene Simmons, Jada Pinkett Smith, Latrell Sprewell, Oliver Stone, Mother Teresa, Trugoy (De La Soul), Blair Underwood, Damon Wayans, Raquel Welch

FASHIZZLE: SNOOP

PERSONIFIES THAT PIMPISH

LIBRA COOL: UNHURRIED,

WELL KEMPT, AND

BRIMMING WITH CHARM.

LIBRA 09.23–10.22

SMOOTH CRIMINAL

THE RUNDOWN

Moment *Johnnie Cochran rhyming in the courtroom: "If it doesn't fit, you must acquit"*

Street occupation/grind *finesse pimp, stripper*

Mix tape *Snoop Dogg, "Beautiful"; Willie Nelson and Julio Iglesias, "To All the Girls I've Loved Before"; No Doubt, "Just a Girl"; Wyclef Jean, "911"; Usher, "Nice and Slow"; Freddie Jackson, "Rock Me Tonight"; Ginuwine, "Same Ol' G"; MC Lyte, "Lyte as a Rock"; Ashanti, "Foolish"*

Best-case scenario *Sting*

Worst-case scenario *Shaggy*

Spot *courtrooms, weddings*

Erogenous zone *luxury hotel*

Vice *indecision*

Natural talent *hosting*

Compatibilites *Aquarius, Aries, Taurus*

GHETTO INDEX

Gangstability	5	
Booty quotient	8	
Bling quotient	6	
Drama quotient	2	
Don status	7	
Trick status	3	
Game quotient	9	
Shiest quotient	8	
Freak quotient	6	

See, Libras know how to use what they got to get what they want. Extra bright, easy on the eyes, well-spoken, and refined, Librafolk got a quiet sort of charisma. Think Snoop Dogg, Marion Jones, Gwen Stefani, and Will Smith. They got the whole package making for some real persuasive maufuckas when they wanna be. Meet them in a bar or something and they'll be standing there under the right lighting flashing you that extra-tartar-control Aquafresh smile. They start speaking with that polite precision, start twinkling in the right places, and then they're razzling and dazzling you with their arsenal of warm laughter, good looks, and great taste and before you know it you been charmed out your socks. And bonds. Resistance is futile. 'Cause like their axis partners, Aries, Libras are very, very good at getting what they want, and if using their looks, lyrics, or the booty does it for them, then so be it. It's the Venusian influence. Like J.J. from *Good Times* used to put it, Well, you know, what can I say?

Smoove. Smooth like melted butter. Smooth like Julio Iglesias. Smooth like Freddie Jackson. Smooth like Usher. And it's not the looks or the humor or the wonderful manners, in truth, that is the key to their power. It's the calculation. Libras got plots and plans. Believe that. Preplanning is Libra's secret technique, something that actually springs from their formidable insecurities. But we'll get back to that. Halfway between the service-oriented analytic perfectionism of Virgo and the intensive, controlling, demanding manipulations of Scorpio,

69

LIBRA

Libra is the intellectual combination of both elements. Libras' lives are often spent struggling to decide which side of themselves to run with. More often than not they don't take a side, choosing instead to vacillate between the two.

We should note here that combining the traits of the two neighboring signs is something all signs do: Sagittarius takes the sexual charge from Scorpio and the ambition of Capricorn; Aquarius takes the emotional disconnect first seen in Capricorn and combines it with Pisces otherworldliness; Cancer retains the lighthearted flightiness of Gemini and develops the generosity that will crescendo in Leo. But because of Libra's vacillation issues, this play between the two sides is particularly intense.

In fact, vacillation is the matter. Libra, the sign of the scales, can't decide whether or not to decide about deciding. Weighing alternatives can become an addiction, a way of avoiding the difficulties and consequences of actually *making a decision.* What results from all the back-and-forth, outside of all the hand-wringing and fretting, is a deep understanding of the issues from both sides. When Libras are asked for their opinion, it is often well-considered and truly helpful. Ask *them* for a decision and things get a little more problematic. Libras would rather get back to twinkling. Keep things light and airy, smiling and winking, without the possible messiness of having to isolate anyone.

Libras' other big weakness is the fact that so many are so vain. (So vain they probably think this whole book is about them.) Mirrors? Plus Libras? Prepare to invest some time watching them watching themselves. Primping, examining, admiring. Then another few hours of primping, examining, and admiring. Wouldn't doubt if Narcissus himself was a Libra. Libra Serena Williams admitted in *Vogue* magazine that she has mirrors all over her bedroom and that there is nothing she likes to do more than stare at herself. When Andre Harrell took over Motown Records he spoke about how important the institution was for

ALL ABOUT APPEARANCES: LIBRAS CONSCIOUSLY DRESS TO IMPRESS. SERENA IN THE CAT SUIT? IMPRESSIVE.

black people. The black Disney, he called it. He then proceeded to launch a multimillion-dollar ad campaign promoting *himself.* "It's On!" read the billboards, featuring himself sitting in a chair. Never mind that he had yet to sign a single act. He was removed from the company in less than a few years.

Part of it too is the Libra aesthetic: clean lines, smooth surfaces, champagne glasses, and gauzy light. Very R&B. Libras like—no, *need*—things to look nice. So vanity kind of goes with that whole thing, if you really think about it. Pretty maufuckers gettin' off from being pretty with other pretty maufuckers in some pretty place, and so on ad infinitum forever and ever, amen. It's enough to make you vomit.

But the main problem that arises from Libra vanity is that Libras be frontin'. Jesus. Fruh-ting. Extra willing to sacrifice the truth to keep up appearances. Role players extraordinaire, Libras are fully aware of their image and will go to great lengths to protect that image. What others think of them can be extremely important to them. A good example is a story a chick with Libra parents told us. She went to visit her extremely sickly father in the hospital wearing a nylon sweat suit. Her father—between fits of coughing, mind you—demanded to know why she would embarrass him by coming "dressed like that." And called the rest of the family from the hospital bed and spread the word. For Libras it's a social thing. They have a deep-seated need to be in with the in crowd. It informs the way they dress, where they go, and who they go with. We know a Libra woman who went thousands of dollars into debt buying shoes and bags, trying to keep up with the fabulous set she was only marginally in. They read many magazines to make sure they are in step with the current trends. Libras will only choose partners they feel would be a good look for them. It's never simply love with Libra. Pretty babies, social positioning, and prestige also figure into their calculations.

None of this speaks enough of how capable this sign is, however. Libras have an uncanny ability to suss information from any and every situation and then act accordingly. They master technique and information. They are not easily fooled. Russell Simmons is a kind of Libra standard in this matter. Watch him work. Cat got his Ph.D. in smooth criminology. For one, he saw very early that hip-hop had universal appeal and promoted, defended, and exploited it from every possible angle. Def Jam, the label he created with Rick Rubin, is now an institution. He has successfully mined the culture's potential for music, fashion, comedy, movies, and now politics. He may be the only nigga alive to have made money off the hip-hop Internet. Russell created the blueprint for the hip-hop mogul. Sean "P. Diddy" Combs of Bad Boy, Jay-Z and Damon Dash of Roc-a-Fella, Master P of No Limit, and Irv Gotti of Murder Inc. all follow directly in his footsteps. Like fellow Libras Ralph Lauren and Donna Karan, Russell Simmons is a trendsetter. When MTV featured him on *Cribs,* he put most of the other folk to shame with his elegant

73

LIBRA

style and taste. A Basquiat-Warhol collaboration hung in his living room, a step up from the framed *Scarface* poster that usually hangs from hip-hop walls. Libras are usually the definers of taste, always up to date and knowledgeable about the history of fashion, politics, and music. Other Libras, like Will Smith, Lyor Cohen, Funkmaster Flex, Don Cornelius, and MC Lyte, are exemplars of how to do your thing and han'le your business.

Libra is the most socially involved of all the signs, so it is natural that the idea of social justice is important to the Libra personality. Facing heavy time and need a lawyer? Get a Libra. In the civic realm they are legal eagles. They make excellent lawyers, judges, and district attorneys. While they may be indecisive and vacillating in their own lives, Libras are dauntless when speaking for others. They are the perfect representatives and can really put the pressure on if they feel an injustice has been done. They are outspoken, sick with the tongue skills, and truly believe in justice and fairness for all. Libra Al Sharpton's lifelong quest to address the inequities in American society is typical of the political activism in Libran blood. (So is his penchant for hairdressing.) Libra Johnnie Cochran, Mr. Dream Team himself, has become famous for his masterful defense of O. J. Simpson, but his skills as an advocate were just as vital in getting the political prisoner Geronimo Pratt released after twenty-six years of false imprisonment.

In other matters: okay, we'll admit that Libras are sexy, if you go for that kind of thing. But again, Libras are fully aware of their sex appeal. Sex is the way to cash in their beauty. Sex is part of their repertoire, but it lacks the passion of, say, the Scorpio's. There is a sense with Libras that they are with you and then again they are not with you. But still sexy. Libras are very sexy people. The thing is that a lot of these cats are not quite as advertised. They can be so into themselves, so caught up in their own looks, that many times they are too distracted to really get down and dirty. Don't get me wrong—Libras will get they freak on, and as with everything else, they have studied up on technique. But some be on the vain shit so hard that even in the midst of a sweaty session they might be too concerned with what all this aggressive movement is doing to their hair. They might have to pass on a position or a sexual experiment out of concern that it might make them look ugly. This is when you gotta grit your teeth and remember *you* chose this maufucka. You was liking all of that hair concern in the restaurant, so now you gotta live with it.

Contenders for the ideal trophy wife, Libra ladies know how to look good and are not above using these skills to further things along. Need homeboy to pay for that weekend in South Beach, Miami? Lemme just show a little leg, drop a button or three. (Occasionally, this fairly straightforward, *Cosmo*-level manipulation can be taken to its hoochie extremes. Let us recall Libra Toni Braxton's sad, desperate attempts to garner J.Lo–level attention at the Grammys.) Sexually insecure, Libra women struggle with a negative body image, despite their attractiveness. They can easily get caught up in following the fashion magazine rules. In fact, they are often "Rules" girls.

The men? Whoo-wee! Can pimp it with the best of them. They be on that Pretty Ricky shit. This is the one man that actually has more beauty products than his woman. The men be kinda fey, to tell the truth. Can come off kinda soft. But the girls love 'em. Like America's favorite gangsta-pimpin' Crip, Snoop Dogg, with his Shirley Temple curls and all, the male Libra appeal is actually the fact that they are so very feminine. It's why Snoop, despite his gangsta profile and lyrics, has always been popular with all sorts. C'mon, Snoop seems too pretty to really come after you with a gun. He strikes a balance of hypermasculine (gangsta) and strangely feminine (sly, fly, and retiring). MC Lyte was able to blend sexual roles in a similar fashion, combining

Brooklyn hardness with feminine dignity. Truth be told, in any successful Libra star one can find that a balance has been struck, be it Will Smith's combination of hip-hop and mainstream humor or Dizzy Gillespie's silly, gregarious persona and very serious musicianship.

Finding that balance is vital for Libra to succeed. Under that capable and glamorous facade is a complex of real emotions. And while they can be extremely subtle and successful in concealing their highly sensitive natures, they are there nonetheless. Strife to a Libra is truly disconcerting. They need peace around them to feel truly secure.

When Libras evolve and do strike that balance, they are capable of intense, joyful, life-affirming, soulful expression. John Coltrane, who suffered from heroin addiction and then kicked the habit and devoted himself completely to his music, was able to create a sound that would inspire and affirm millions of people all over the world for years to come. There is even a church dedicated to his music. When Libras use their talents to serve rather than self-serve, they begin to shine in an entirely different, more ethereal kind of light.

THE INFAMOUS

Debbie Allen, Pedro Almodóvar, Amiri Baraka, Chuck Berry, Lorraine Bracco, Toni Braxton, Shirley Caesar, Tisha Campbell, Johnnie Cochran, Lyor Cohen, John Coltrane, Don Cornelius, Jermaine Dupri, Eminem, Funkmaster Flex, Gandhi, Dizzy Gillespie, Ginuwine, Mean Joe Greene, Dick Gregory, Bryant Gumbel, Daryl Hall, Andre Harrell, Donny Hathaway, Evander Holyfield, Julio Iglesias, Freddie Jackson, Jesse Jackson, Tito Jackson, Wyclef Jean, Beverly Johnson, Marion Jones, Donna Karan, Ralph Lauren, Marley Marl, Wynton Marsalis, MC Lyte, Terry McMillan, Isaac Mizrahi, Thelonious Monk, Elijah Muhammad, Mya, Olivia Newton-John, Sharon Osbourne, Scottie Pippen, Bud Powell, Anne Rice, Jerry Rice, Bobby Seale, Shaggy, Ntozake Shange, Al Sharpton, Russell Simmons, Will Smith, Snoop Dogg, Gwen Stefani, Sting, Peter Tosh, Desmond Tutu, Usher, Ben Vereen, Serena Williams, Demond Wilson (Lamont from *Sanford and Son*)

POWER

OF THE P:

EVE EXUDES THE SEXUAL

CONFIDENCE TYPICAL OF

THE SCORPIO WOMAN.

SCORPIO 10.23–11.21

FREAK LIKE ME

THE RUNDOWN

feminine, *fixed, water*

Motto *I desire*

Sound bite *"Ooo, baby I like it raw"* *(Ol Dirty Bastard)*

Ruling planet *Mars, Pluto*

Color *burgundy*

Rock *topaz*

Physical *sex organs*

Icon *Dracula*

Genius *Pablo Picasso*

Beverage *tequila*

Guilty pleasure *turning you out and sucking you dry*

Accessory *stilettos*

Ride *Bentley Continental GT*

Find them *in the VIP section*

Visual Goodfellas

THE RUNDOWN

Moment *Demi Moore rolls to a movie premiere with her boytoy and her ex-husband*

Street occupation/grind *hired gun*

Mix tape *Nas and Diddy, "Hate Me Now"; Eve, "Gangsta Lovin'"; Ol' Dirty Bastard, "Raw"; Sisqó, "Thong Song"; Fabolous, "Keepin' It Gangsta"; Adina Howard, "Freak Like Me"; Nelly, "Hot in Herre"*

Best-case scenario *Mahalia Jackson*

Worst-case scenario *Ol' Dirty Bastard*

Spot *New Orleans, Trinidad and Tobago*

Erogenous zone *dungeon*

Vice *vengeance*

Natural talents *freakin' and creepin'*

Compatibilities *Capricorn, Leo, Pisces*

GHETTO INDEX

Gangstability	9	
Booty quotient	8	
Bling quotient	6	
Drama quotient	5	
Don status	7	
Trick status	3	
Game quotient	9	
Shiest quotient	8	
Freak quotient	8	

Understanding the Scorpio is recognizing that these sexified, passionate, intense maufuckas are wired for power. Balls of pressurized energy bustin' out their pores. Not a game. Not to be played with. Vampire gangstas. Gangsta vampires. Scorpios exploit every opportunity and every possibility. They take advantage. Even if it's to their disadvantage. Can't help it. It's like the story of the scorpion and the frog. Scorpion was injured, needed to get across a deep pond. Asked Frog to swim him across the pond. Frog refused, citing the fact that Scorpion was known to sting maufuckas. "Why would I do that?" Scorpion replied. "You'd be doing me a favor. Besides, if you're swimming me across and I sting you, we would both drown." Finally consenting, Frog warily allowed Scorpion on his back and began to swim across. Just as Frog reached the deepest part of the pond, he felt a hot burning sensation in his leg. Scorpion stuck his stinger deep into Frog, paralyzing him. Frog, struggling to stay afloat, realized death was certain. As they slowly started to sink under the pond water, Frog asked Scorpion why he would doom them both. "It's just my nature," Scorpion replied.

See, Scorpio gangsta is a particular brand of gangsta. There's the two-fisted kind, bustin' down doors, gettin' blood on his hands, and working the fear angle (see Aries, page 3). Then there's the subtle gangsta who rarely breaks a sweat, does all his dirt third person, and controls situations from behind closed doors. Scorpio's more the lat-

THAT JUST MY BABYDADDY: FATHER OF FOURTEEN KIDS, DRUG ADDICT, ALCOHOLIC, AND MOST UNLIKELY POP STAR, OL' DIRTY BASTARD, A.K.A. DIRT MCGIRT, EXEMPLIFIES SCORPIO POWERS RUN AMOK.

ter. Like the other water signs, Cancer and Pisces, Scorpios are manipulators who can slay you in the details. They stay running shit. We recall a Scorpio businesswoman who ran a PR company with her husband. She demanded a client pay their firm more than the usual rate for an upcoming project. Mind you, she used to sleep with the client before she got married. When the client balked, citing the husband's slack work habits, she pulled out the Scorpio arsenal. In the weeks following she, one, made her request an all-or-nothing proposition, threatening to pull out completely and drop the client; two, stopped having sex with her husband until he got his work done faster; and three, threatened to make her husband quit and get a higher-paying job elsewhere. Needless to say, she got the account and the loot. How? The power of the p-u-s-s-y. Sex is a weapon Scorpios wield with deftness.

Even when not a gangsta per se, the Scorpio needs control of his or her surroundings to feel safe. This preoccupation with control is rooted in deep-seated insecurities and a primordial need for nurturing. Scorpios can be intensely possessive and struggle with jealousy throughout their lives. Some may get on some stalker-type shit or partake of volatile, self-destructive behavior. Still, this is all on the surface. Below the sur-

CAN'T STOP, WON'T STOP: P. DIDDY'S CAREER HAS BEEN A LONG DANCE WITH DEATH. EVEN WHEN BESET WITH DIFFICULTIES, SCORPIOS MANAGE TO EMERGE FROM TRAGEDY UNFAZED.

face, they can be emotionally fearful, fragile, and insecure. Their lives are often marred by early trauma, such as dealing with death and loss, that forges an intense nature and forces them in later years into deep soul-searching. Their infamous tempers are the remains of childhoods fraught with pain and confusion. Though they're capable of boiling over in violent displays of bitterness, jealousy, and possessiveness, truth is these firelike water signs have hidden depths of real sensitivity—which very few get to see. When they find love, they are generous, nurturing, and wonderful to their families. But hurt them and it's all about the git back. Woe unto you! When Tupac moaned, "Revenge is like the sweetest joy next to getting pussy" on "Hail Mary," he described the lower Scorpio disposition to a T. Scorpio Charles Bronson, who made like a thousand vigilante films, was a natural at the role. Vengeance often becomes the primary motivation spurring Scorpios to great achievement. Sean Combs got his nickname, Puff Daddy, from the children in his neighborhood finding a cruel way to call him soft. He turned the insult into a household name.

It's exactly when you think you've conquered the scorpion that you are in the most danger. They thrive on the seemingly insurmountable. Yeah, you believe it's over. Puff is a classic case. Puffy's entire career has been marked by a kind of against-all-odds patterning, an ongoing dance with death. His father's early demise, his CCNY event that ended in the tragic death of several attendees, Biggie's death, and various shootings and murders have haunted him throughout his life. Many of these incidents seemed career-threatening. Yet, in true Scorpio fashion, he emerged from these crises stronger, more secure in his stardom.

Scorpios can party to the edge of death. Getting drunk and high, indulging every sensual desire, can become an addiction if they are not careful. Need we point to the wild-ass Scorpio poster chile, Ol' Dirty Bastard? Scorpios can keep it carnal when they want to. Sex, alcohol, drugs, sex, and sex can easily become modus operandi for the scorpion. Ol' Dirty Bastard, once referred to as the id of hip-hop, exemplifies the dark extremes of the Scorpio persona: drug abuse, alcoholism, and near-death experiences are recurring themes in his life, even as he maintains a charismatic hold on thousands of fans. Scorpios are passionate, at times to a fault, but it's all or nothing. All that said, Scorpios are among the most self-aware cats you'll ever come across. Most know their limitations and act accordingly.

You can recognize many a Scorpio by their sharp features: nostrils, nose, and eyebrows. Their eyes might be slightly droopy, with a sensuous mouth perpetually bent in a crooked, sly-ass smile. The women got body: either in that buxom Mae West/B Angie B direction or that taut and wiry Lisa Bonet way. Sexually uninhibited, they have bodies that, in the words of the "Ar-ruh" Kelly, seem like they're ready. Odd-looking though they may be, Scorpios cast a spell on their victi— eh-hemm, err, ah, fans—with a combination of nerve, provocation, and hypnotics. Eve, the rap diva, is typical in that whatever she may lack in prototypical physical beauty she more than compensates for with sexual confidence. Like the Scorpic city of New Orleans, there's somethin' real hoodoo about the lot of 'em. Voodoo chill'un. As P. Diddy once put it, they have the power to make you love them. How else could you explain a strange-looking chick like Julia Roberts reigning over Hollywood as America's pretty woman? You can also recognize Scorpios by their innate sense of style. Always current and in fashion, they naturally cultivate a sultry look that only adds to their game. Scorpios are endowed with that Dracula charm: fly, seductive, talking that good shit in your ear even while they drain the very life out of you.

They have an instinctual, almost psychic ability to know who got the power, how to get it, and what to do with it once it's got. Think about Senator Hillary Clinton. From early on, chick overlooked her husband's pussy-chasin' ways in order to fulfill her plans for both of them. And while many Scorpions are not above fucking their way to the top, Scorpios rank among the most hardworking and on-point professionals in existence. Scorpios will ruthlessly and efficiently do whatever is necessary to achieve the desired result. It should be noted that the richest man in the world, Bill Gates, is a Scorpio. Many millionaires are.

Scorpio rules the sex organs, which might help explain why so many are loath to wear underwear. Scorpion Sisqó celebrated the thong in song and named his album after his nickname for his own genitalia. (*Unleash the Dragon.* Get it?) Sexually, Scorpios have an overflow of energy. Prone to bisexuality, both the men and the women,

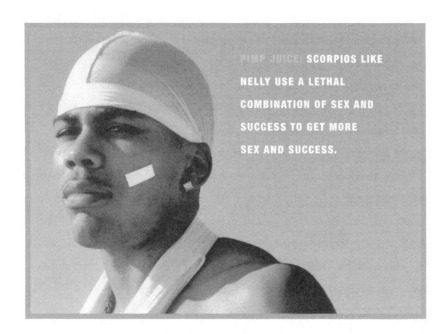

PIMP JUICE: SCORPIOS LIKE NELLY USE A LETHAL COMBINATION OF SEX AND SUCCESS TO GET MORE SEX AND SUCCESS.

they demand plenty of stimulation and challenge—toys, porn movies, or any other sex aids available. Naturally dominating, they don't mind getting tied up or the feeling of leather, latex, and rubber. As with their sistren on the Taurus-Scorpio axis, money can also move them to erotic extremes.

But they be on that shit from birth. We know a three-year-old Scorpio who is already showing certain tendencies kinda early. Like one time, her moms walked in and caught her spanking herself in the mirror. Mom, in shock, asks, "Why are you spanking yourself in the mirror?" The girl turned and said, " 'Cause I like it!" It is only just beginning.

The crazy shit about Scorpio is that for all the ruthless, conniving sex-crazed behavior often associated with the sign, there is also a deeply spiritual nature. There are three stages of the Scorp: the scorpion, the phoenix, and the eagle. It begins with the scorpion—sexual, destructive, and enslaved by its own desire. Once the soul evolves out of the lower nature, the scorpion is burned and rises from the ashes transformed. Scorpio signifies death, but also rebirth. It is this phoenix aspect that gives the Scorpio the capacity to overcome anything. The poison that does not kill Scorpios makes them stronger. And transforms them. Many Scorpios will in later years transform their enormous sexual energy into a daunting religious fervor. Gospel singer Mahalia Jackson, evangelist Billy Graham, and Protestant reformer Martin Luther typify the extent to which Scorpios can go once they catch the spirit.

On a spiritual level, Scorpio stands at the gates of the advanced trials awaiting the human soul in the four remaining signs of the zodiac: Sagittarius, Capricorn, Aquarius, and Pisces. If the scorpion learns its lessons, survives the trials of the phoenix, and makes the full evolution, it becomes the eagle: a keen-eyed achiever and leader with noble bearings. Even if Scorpios don't manage such exalted soul growth, they are still likely to achieve "Freak of the Week" accolades from some amateur porn site. Something they could be quite proud of, we're sure.

THE INFAMOUS

Björk, Lisa Bonet, Charles Bronson, Hillary Clinton, William "Bootsy" Collins, Sean "P. Diddy" Combs, Dorothy Dandridge, Sandi "Pepa" Denton, Bo Derek, Leonardo DiCaprio, Eve, Fabolous, Calista Flockhart, Larry Flynt, Jodie Foster, Daisy Fuentes, Whoopi Goldberg, John Gotti, Billy Graham, Ken Griffey, Jr., Tonya Harding, Mahalia Jackson, Peter Jackson (director, *Lord of the Rings*), Bobby Knight, Leadbelly, Nia Long, Martin Luther, Charles Manson, Whitman "Grady" Mayo, Jenny McCarthy, Demi Moore, Brittany Murphy, Nelly, Ol' Dirty Bastard, Kelly and Jack Osbourne, Pelé, Pablo Picasso, Dana Plato, Minnie Riperton, Julia Roberts, Roseanne, Run, RuPaul, Winona Ryder, Scarface, Martin Scorsese, Roxanne Shanté, Sinbad, Sisqó, Sammy Sosa, Bram Stoker, Ted Turner, Ivana Trump, Gabrielle Union, Owen Wilson

TEFLON DON:

SAGITTARIAN HUSTLERS

LIKE DON KING

AND PABLO ESCOBAR

COMBINE DEVASTATING

MOUTH GAME WITH

COLD-HEARTED

RUTHLESSNESS.

SAGITTARIUS 11.22–12.21

KEEPIN' IT GANGSTA

THE RUNDOWN

masculine, *mutable, fire*

Motto *I see*

Sound bite *"Bite my tongue for no one" (Notorious B.I.G.)*

Ruling planet *Jupiter*

Color *purple*

Rock *turquoise*

Physical *hips and thighs*

Icon *centaur*

Genius *Jimi Hendrix*

Beverage *Belvedere*

Guilty pleasure *intellectual beatdowns*

Accessory *global phone*

Ride *Lamborghini*

Find them *at the casino*

Visual What's Love Got to Do With It

Moment *Hendrix lighting his guitar on fire during performance*

THE RUNDOWN

Street occupation/grind *training pit bulls; the connect*

Mix tape *Jay-Z,* Reasonable Doubt; *Naughty by Nature, "Ghetto Bastard"; Christina Aguilera, "Dirrty"; Tina Turner, "Private Dancer"; Britney Spears, "I'm a Slave 4 U"; Trina, "Da Baddest Bitch"; Frank Sinatra, "My Way"; Trick Daddy feat. Trina, "Nann"*

Best-case scenario *Bruce Lee*

Worst-case scenario *Richard Pryor*

Spot *Detroit*

Erogenous zone *the park after dark*

Vice *talkin' greazy*

Natural talent *selling anything*

Compatibilities *Gemini, Aries, Virgo*

GHETTO INDEX

Gangstability	10
Booty quotient	9
Bling quotient	6
Drama quotient	8
Don status	8
Trick status	3
Game quotient	9
Shiest quotient	5
Freak quotient	9

Wild horses. Every one of 'em. Sag maufuckas be off the chain. A dynamic combination of wild-ass spirituality and on-point gangsterism. They be on some real life Dr. Jekyll and Mr. Hyde shit. They might be the nicest people you ever met in your life: magnetic, good-natured, laughing, and joking. Then out of nowhere they'll come out their face. "I'm just saying, you look like you can't fuck." Or "Shit, momma, you got fat in all the wrong places." If candor could kill, youknowwhatwe-sayin'? Those little hesitations we might feel before sayin' some ol' crazy shit do not exist for the Sagittarius. With Sag, it comes out their mouth as it comes in their head. Unfiltered. Served up raw with a smile.

Most Sagittarius folks come from the can't-take-the-heat-get-the-fuck-out-the-kitchen school of thought. Add to that the fact that they see it as their divine duty to keep it hot and you have the basics on Sag public behavior. Now, this need to maintain the heat has its good and bad sides. For one, the party don't start till the Sag gets there. Masters of the bold move, archers know how to grab the spotlight and are perfectly happy to set shit off. These are highly sociable party people. Got jokes for days. Interestingly enough, Sagittarians, in spite of all the carousing they might be involved in, are rather sophisticated. Reason being, Sags are high-frequency elite minds who don't suffer fools gladly. Sagittarius Jay-Z, for example, is considered a party rapper by most so-called hip-hop heads. Truth is, he is one of the most intelligent rappers ever to record, but he was forced to dumb down his rhymes because a good portion of what he was saying was flying over people's heads. In the beginning of his career, especially on *Reasonable Doubt,* his raps were weighted with double and triple meanings, razor-sharp observations, and intricate rhyme patterns few party people could appreciate. The level of sophistication was lost on most, so he was forced to take it down a notch, offering a song with the artistic intensity of his first record once in a blue moon. Sagittarian males might be the cats in the zodiac who can reference Dostoyevsky while destroying you in a Madden football game and sipping on some Ballantine's. Sagittarian females might be the women that will kick it with a guy, outthink, outdance, and outdrink him. Take him home then kick him out an hour later 'cause his sex technique wasn't interesting. They just like that.

The thing is, while they can be the ones to make a party live, they can just as easily be the ones to deaden the whole shit. Sag will be that cat taking the broken champagne bottle to a nigga's neck. The women too. Like Jay-Z once said about himself, they're the type to overdo it. Get some stimulants in these high-strung cats and you are literally playing with fire. Once Treach, the Sag leader of Naughty by Nature, got mad at his boss at the record company about a money issue. Next day he ran up in the office and dropped a bag of snakes on her desk. With a Sag, things can go any which way. But they wild out with rea-son. There's always a reason.

Archers are always in danger of doing too much. Take, for exam-ple, Sagittarius ingenue Christina Aguilera's overwrought dress code. Let's be honest: chick is gifted, the voice is next level. But if there was ever anyone truly in need of a stylist . . . But that's that the Sag shit. Superheroes in their own minds. Many a Sag will show up in an outfit made for the comic books. And while it may be wild and unlike anything you've ever seen, it will undoubtedly have its own internal logic that demonstrates their ambition and expresses their creativity. Think of world-record holder Flo-Jo and her ghetto long nails and her one-legged tracksuits. Turned into a perfect marketing maneuver. Better yet, think Bruce Lee. Gangsta! Sagittarius all day. His charisma, hot-ass outfits (Bruce used to rock them Chinese slippers like they were gators!), lightning quickness, athletic prowess, and soul brother atti-

tude are all marks of the archer's ways and actions. Even his early death was in line with Sagittarian nature. Time moves fast with Sagittarius.

You can recognize the Sagittarius by his or her longish face and perpetual energy. The last of the fire signs, Sags can't stop. Won't stop. You can often hear the crackle of fire in

BADOONKADOONK: SAG FEMALES LIKE TINA, BRITNEY, AND TRINA TEND TO BE BOOTYLICIOUS.

their voices. Sagittarian singers Lou Rawls, Dionne Warwick, Frank Sinatra, and Tina Turner all have that certain rasp that makes their voices distinctive. Physically, they resemble the superheroes they fancy themselves to be. Sagittarius got body. The men are usually well-defined and athletic. The women, like the men, have lots of shoulder and muscular thighs. Some Sags, like Leos, can be on the thick side, al-

ways seemingly on the verge of getting fat. In the same way that many Leos actually look feline and Pisces have fishlike qualities, Sagittarians physically resemble horses. But shhhexy all the same.

Which brings us to the other thing about the majority of Sag females: ass for days. They be packing! Sag raptress Trina is known for her booty. Don't sleep: Tina Turner was, er, is still

FEEL THE FIRE:

INVENTIVE, BOLD, AND RUNNIN' WILD, HENDRIX, LIKE MOST SAGITTARIANS, TOOK CREATIVITY TO THE HILT.

holdin' too. Think them legs stopped at her thigh? It's the horse in them. Even Britney Spears got a little sumthin' sumthin' happenin' back there.

And oooo, these maufuckers be slingin' it. Both the men and women are working with torrid sexuality. Nonstop energy and ready for anything. Sag got libido for days with ego to match. Willing and able to do anything you can conceive of: candles, handcuffs, multiple partners, acrobatics, swings, what have you. The Sagittarius be 'bout it.

Like all fire signs, Sag has an aggressive streak, an uncontrolled side that is a manifestation of that beast living inside. (It's why Sags connect with animals. Think DMX and his complete identification with pit bulls.) It is the driving force behind their success. Sags won't take no for an answer, and in most cases that means they get what they're aiming for. Sagittarians are incredible salesmen. A few minutes with a Sag and you're signed up for a shoddy year-long cell-phone plan, wearing ugly glasses you didn't want or need, and holding a bag of magic beans. By the time Sag is done speed-talking and provoking, there's no time to protest or even nurture your doubts.

Relationships with these types are a trip. Freedom-loving and adventurous, they are a dynamic combination of spirituality and gangsterism. The women can be mannish in the way they go about their sexual business, but they also have an innate understanding of the power of slavery. She can completely prostrate herself in order to draw a man in. Dedicate herself wholly to his whim. He's thinking shit is sweet; but Sags crave power, and those dynamics can be flipped real quick. Ask Ike Turner, he'll tell you: the Sag woman might lay down, but they ain't gonna stay down. Believe that. Tina Turner is an exemplary Sag story. Her energetic, downright church-fire style of dancing and singing brought her to fame with her controlling, abusing Scorpio husband, Ike. He was whopping her ass. But once she found herself and left him, she grew in both stature and power.

But again, Sags' intelligence is their most lethal weapon—it's broad, versatile. Like their Gemini brethren, Sags can talk with authority on race-car motors, ska music, or *Star Wars* trivia without even thinking about it. Like a wild horse, the Sag mind needs open fields in which to run. Focusing and choosing just one field of interest is a struggle for Sag, and often is the difference between ultimate success or failure.

Sags also have a gangsta intelligence that can determine who got the power and what the state of the game is at any point in time. They're arguably the most gangsta of the zodiac, because they are equal parts intellect and instinct. Ruthless and ambitious, these are the last maufuckers you want after you when they're highly evolved. Pablo Escobar, perhaps the greatest outlaw of the last century, was the prototypical Sagittarius. He ruled Colombia and his cocaine cartel with a simple rule: the silver or the bullet. In other words, he either bought you out or killed you. If he bought you out, then you were to do his will for the rest of your life. If he killed you, well, you were just out of his way. It was highly effective, and it maintained his vise-grip on Colombia and its cocaine trade for years.

See, it's typical for Sags to bully their way through opposition. They use mental and physical speed and force to get what they want. Sometimes that backfires and they move too fast, making too many presumptions. But they move by instinct, and most of the time they're dead on. Sagittarian Adam Clayton Powell, Jr., moved with a gangsta's boldness and held down Harlem for nearly a decade. A highly popular preacher and politician, he was also known to frequent pool halls and juke joints. His ability to do as he pleased was un-

precedented in such high-level politics. He was the true definition of a player in his era. Still don't buy Sag's gangsta credentials? Two words: Don King.

Sagittarians like Don King approach life with a charismatic abandon and an almost mystical ability to transform everything around them. They are both magnetic and destructive. They're competitive to a fault, and pain can turn into the ultimate challenge for them, a cruel reminder that they are alive. Sometimes they become addicted to the pain and the violent requirements for overcoming it. In Greek mythology, there is a story of a centaur who gets stuck in a massive thornbush. As the thorns impale him, he kicks and bucks only to be impaled again and again. Bloody, enraged, and drunk from the pain, he snaps at anyone

99

SAGITTARIUS

who tries to help. Psychologically, Sag is prone to falling into painful and cyclical traps.

Sags are creative even in their self-destruction. Think Richard Pryor, DMX, Sammy Davis, Jr., Jimi Hendrix. They go all out. It's the fire in them. Take Hendrix. If there is gonna be a psychedelic electric bluesman burning guitars on stage—shit, playing it with his teeth—he's gonna be a Sag. Jimi Hendrix's fiery abandon on the electric guitar and in life is a clear example.

What it comes down to is the Sag lives and dies by his ego. And therein lies the problem. Despite Sagittarians' amazing abilities, their ego often blinds them to the real situation. If Sagittarians could wean themselves off the ego, learn the virtue and value of humility, and apply a bit of it to their day-to-day existence, then that boundless potential, that spiritual victory they ultimately seek and that is their birthright, would be truly achieved. If not, the Sag will probably opt to go out in a blaze of glory, teeth clenched and bustin' shots at that ass. Real superherolike.

THE INFAMOUS

Christina Aguilera, Anita Baker, Tyra Banks, Tyson Beckford, Winston Churchill, Crazy Horse, Sammy Davis, Jr., Joe DiMaggio, DMX, morning-show radio jock Dr. Dre, Sheila E., Pablo Escobar, Jamie Foxx, Redd Foxx, Nelly Furtado, Robin Givens, Elián González, Green Arrow, Florence Griffith-Joyner, Bob Guccione, Jimi Hendrix, Billy Idol, Jermaine Jackson, Samuel L. Jackson, Jay-Z, John F. Kennedy, Don King, Kurupt, Bruce Lee, Little Richard, Lucy Liu, Alyssa Milano, Jim Morrison, Baby Face Nelson, Sinéad O'Connor, Ozzy Osbourne, Brad Pitt, Adam Clayton Powell, Jr., Lou Rawls, Bart Simpson, Frank Sinatra, Britney Spears, Treach, Trick Daddy, Trina, Tina Turner, Mo Vaughn, Gianni Versace, Dionne Warwick, Flip Wilson

HIGHEST HIGHS, LOWEST LOWS: EXTREME JOY AND PAIN FELT BY CAPRICORNS IS REFLECTED IN CAP R. KELLY'S HEARTFELT SONGS.

CAPRICORN 12.22–01.19

THE HARD ROAD

THE RUNDOWN

feminine, *cardinal, earth*

Motto *I use*

Sound bite *"I've been to the mountaintop." (Rev. Dr. Martin Luther King, Jr.)*

Ruling planet *Saturn*

Color *dark green, brown*

Rock *garnet*

Physical *knees, bones, teeth*

Icon *Muhammad Ali*

Genius *Martin Luther King, Jr.*

Beverage *Cristal*

Guilty pleasure *working too damn much*

Accessory *dark sunglasses*

Ride *Range Rover 4.6*

Find them *at the bank*

Visual *Mahogany*

Moment *Frazier flooring Ali in the last round of their first fight*

THE RUNDOWN

Street occupation/grind *clocker*

Mix tape *Slick Rick, "Children's Story"; Clipse, "Grindin'";*
Mary J. Blige, "My Life"; R. Kelly, R.; Sade, Diamond Life;
LL Cool J, "Mama Said Knock You Out"; Aaliyah, "Try Again";
Gwen Guthrie, "Padlock"; Wu-Tang Clan, "C.R.E.A.M.";
Raekwon, "Incarcerated Scarfaces"

Best-case scenario *Aaliyah*

Worst-case scenario *Idi Amin*

Spot *Chicago*

Erogenous zone *office, late at night*

Vice *workaholic*

Natural talent *survival*

Compatibilities *Taurus, Scorpio, Leo*

GHETTO INDEX

Gangstability	9	
Booty quotient	5	
Bling quotient	6	
Drama quotient	8	
Don status	8	
Trick status	4	
Game quotient	7	
Shiest quotient	4	
Freak quotient	8	

Capricorns are the hard-workingest maufuckers in the zodiac. It's a sickness, really. It's like they can't get enough of it. Reason being? Capricorns revere achievement. Getting it done is their greatest joy in life. It's all about climbing that mountain. Getting to the top no matter the terrain or the obstacles. Their symbol, the goat-fish, is a mythical creature that can travel the entire expanse of the material world, from sea floor to mountaintop. It can reach the highest heights and the lowest lows. That is where Capricorns go. As the last of the earth signs, Capricorn shows us the concluding lessons of the material realm: the virtue of work, the reality and necessity of limitations, and the science of how to utilize material in the service of others.

See, Caps love positions of power. At the top is where they see themselves. As natural-born leaders, they dictate what must get done with an air of confidence, sometimes arrogance, that comes from the experience and hard work it took to get them there.

Caps who aren't CEOs of companies or managers in the professional realm tend to be group leaders in their social circles. In this position they floss in a much more quiet way than their fellow earth-sign Taureans. High-end clothing designers on their back, the best car they can get on the lot, beautiful things in the home—all are necessary status symbols for Caps. The men seek trophy wives they can connect to in a real way, while the women are generally attracted to the Donald Trump type. Or the neighborhood drug kingpin.

For the Capricorn, it is not about the possession as much as what the possession represents. While they may have certain bling tendencies (a Capricorn is not opposed to getting iced up or designered out), the little extras are more a reminder of how far they've come. With this, they tend to have a bad case of keepin' up with the Joneses. But more often than not, all the valuables they accumulate over the years end up piled up in a room somewhere, collecting dust and crowding up their houses. It's an earth-sign disease and a security thing: Caps live in fear that the thing they throw out today might suddenly become necessary tomorrow. The pileup might be a sign of something the Capricorn must remain vigilant against: stagnation. Caps go both ways: either they are extremely neat or they are all over the place. Generally patient and

FIGHT OF THE CENTURY: IN THE GRITTY BATTLES BETWEEN THESE TWO CAPS, ALI AND FRAZIER BOTH DUG DEEP AND REFUSED TO LET UP, BRINGING OUT THE BEST IN EACH OTHER.

focused, Capricorns keep their eyes on the prize. Rarely do they get sidetracked. It's only when something seriously gets in the way (problems paying tuition, having a child earlier than planned, not landing that ideal job) that they can sink into deep depression. Or when their better qualities are unnoticed or underappreciated. They may stay in the house for weeks, not answer the phone, go underground. But the Cap is too invested in the struggle to completely give in. It's only a matter of time before they resume their workaholic ways.

There are, as with all zodiac signs, those Caps who play against type. Some Capricorns shun material possessions and live like hermits in a spiritual world of their own making. This type can be likened to the wise old man in the mountain whom everyone in the village comes to for wisdom and great advice but who has chosen not to live among society.

Capricorns opt for the hard road. They take on suffering without blinking. They're the kind to do more work for less pay, believing—no, knowing—that they will get theirs in the end. The kind to bear heavy burdens physically, emotionally, and spiritually. We tellin' you: Caps be going *through* it. Mary J. Blige is a classic case. Brought up in Yonkers, Mary developed her singing style with her friends in the projects. Discovered by Andre Harrell, she had a raw, beautiful voice and style. Nurtured by Sean "Puffy" Combs, she became an instant hit. But even as she had number-one records on the charts, she was still struggling in the projects. She soon got involved in a disastrous love affair with K-Ci of Jodeci and began to drink and do drugs heavily. Still reeling from heartbreak, she documented her pain on her second album, *My Life,* and cemented her position as this generation's soul queen. Pulling herself out of depression and self-loathing, she used music to turn her tragedy into triumph, releasing three more albums. With each

one her fan base grew and her outlook became more and more positive. Once rejected as too ghetto for mainstream acceptance, she is now seen as a card-carrying member of America's glitterati. It's the typical Capricorn story: rejection transformed into acceptance, difficulties surmounted, and perseverance overcoming resistance.

Time is on their side, though. These are folks with staying power. The saying that God doesn't give you any burden that you cannot handle applies to these folks. They are patient and have been gifted with enormous stamina to weather life's storms. Some Capricorns are brought down so low exactly because they are capable of the highest achievements.

A Capricorn like LL Cool J defies all hip-hop laws in terms of staying power. Cat is like the last man standing. He has maintained his star power in a notoriously fickle environment. Hiphop eats its artists alive. Most rappers have a shelf life of two years, tops. But LL is on his third decade in the game. He is an old-school legend, a hip-hop icon and niggra's still making hits. Caps got that goat-stamina. Maybe that's why he claimed the title G.O.A.T. (Greatest of All Time).

Like their opposites on the axis, Cancerians, Capricorns have emotions that run so deep that words often fail them. While Cancers will channel their sadness by running home to momma, Caps keep it to themselves and keep going with their heads held high as if nothing's wrong. Communication is sometimes difficult for them. They prefer silence to random chatter. When they do speak (oftentimes with bleating voices), it is usually with real eloquence. Martin Luther King, Jr., is one of the best examples of the rhetorical heights Caps can reach when communicating. His "I Have a Dream" speech is among the greatest spoken-word performances in American history.

Still, a good number of Capricorns don't deal with their pain, concealing their feelings and experiences. Conceal? Make that repress. Blame it on Saturn, their ruling planet. For one, the Capricorn private life is just that: private. Never really hear Capricorn business in the street. They do their dirt all by their lonely. But two, they work out their trauma alone. Unfortunately, it often builds up inside them, until either their health begins to suffer or they become some miserable bastards to live or work with.

Capricorns have a higher capacity for cruelty because often they are so cruel to themselves. The pressure they put on themselves to take whatever they're into to the next level drives them crazy. They can be especially hard on those they love. You get an exemption if you're a baby, however.

The thing is, Capricorns are adults as children and become children as adults—only when they're with children do they begin to live out their youth. (But know that once you hit age ten or thereabouts, Cap's gloves come off.) Capricorn Idi Amin, a soldier and top-ranked boxer who became dictator of Uganda, perpetrated some extreme cruelties on his political enemies: torture and imprisonment, and some said if he really wasn't feelin' you, you might become part of his evening meal. But the misery Caps cause others has everything to do with the misery they experience themselves. Woe to those poor souls with an unhappy Capricorn boss. Dickens's character Ebenezer Scrooge was the classic example of the miserable Capricorn who needs to trace the roots of his own suffering to understand why he is such a merciless slave driver.

The secret to really understanding Capricorns is in their music. Check their CD collection. The story is told. Words are not enough to express the depth of their feelings. Only music comes close to doing their emotions justice. Sade, R. Kelly,

NO MORE DRAMA: IN TRUE CAP FASHION, MARY J. TRANSFORMED HER DIFFICULTIES IN LOVE AND LIFE INTO HARD-WON SUCCESS.

Mary J. Blige, Aaliyah, and other Cap musicians all tap the unspoken feelings that reside in the Capricorn heart. Consider Mary's *My Life* or Sade's *Stronger Than Pride* or Aaliyah's *One in a Million.* That solemn sound, that lonely plea edged with pathos, is the sound of the Capricorn heart.

Beneath their cool, detached demeanor lies a soft heart within extremely thick skin. Tough. It is why so many excel at physical activities like boxing. George Foreman, Roy Jones, Jr., Joe Frazier, and Muhammad Ali were all born under Capricorn. Some of the greatest fights in the history of the sport were a result of that Capricorn determination and toughness. The three fights between Ali and Frazier were epic battles precisely because neither Capricorn—they happen to share the same birthday—would roll over. They went at each other with everything for hours. Ali's jaw got broke. Frazier was beat up so bad he couldn't come out of his corner. It was a major clash of two tremendous hearts and wills.

Caps hold tightly to their principles. Muhammad Ali stayed true to his Islamic faith and refused the draft even though it meant losing his title and his prime boxing years. Martin Luther King, of course, would be stabbed and threatened and bombed for his outspoken stance against segregation and racism, but his dogged determination to transform American society made him an American hero. Capricorns are likely to have their own private relationship with God. This is their main source of strength, providing structure to lives often confronted with chaos.

Saturn, their rigid ruling planet, makes Capricorns clear about what they will and won't do. While Sagittarians are hard-pressed to see any limit to their power and possibilities, Caps see nothing but. Regulations are where they begin. And like trying to pull a goat that does not want to move, it is damn near impossible to force a Cap to do what a Cap does not want to do. It's like asking Al Sharpton to cut off that permed coiffed bouffant 'do he's known for. Not gonna happen. Like their earth-sign brethren and sistren, Taurus and Virgo, Caps are slow to change and stubborn as fuck. They live by hard and fast rules that they are loath to break.

But don't get it twisted, Caps ain't no saints. Chicago's most notorious gangster, Al Capone, for example, was a stone cold Capricorn. Plus, these cats be gittin' down. If they do party, they party hard. Drink hard. Drug hard. Undercover freaks, quiet as it's kept. Capricorn Luther Campbell of 2 Live Crew used to get his thing sucked on stage on a regular basis. R. Kelly. (Need we mention the triple-X DVD?) Bona-fide freak. If you listened to the lyrics to Aaliyah's "Rock the Boat" you'd peep it in her too. Caps got a lot of pent-up everything, so when it is finally let out, run for cover. Capricorns will put the *d* in debauchery.

The truth is that Caps have a dark side. When they tap into it, it is uncontrolled, it can overtake their entire being. In fact, Mr. Dark Side himself, Darth Vader, is a morality tale for the Capricorn personality. Early tragedy made him give in to his pent-up frustrations and turned him into a powerful, high-ranking cyborg, alien to himself and his loved ones, a slave to his ambition. It was only when he placed his power in the service of his family and not his work that his soul was redeemed.

The key to Capricorns' evolution is to balance out the rigid aspects of their personalities and become more flexible. Learn to not make pain and limitation their only reality. If they can do that, Capricorns gain an eternal youthfulness, becoming younger as they get older. If not, they are likely to live alone, age prematurely, suffer from arthritis, live in a stuffy house crowded with too many possessions, and scare the neighborhood children when they walk by.

THE INFAMOUS

Aaliyah, Alvin Ailey, Muhammad Ali, Idi Amin, Soul II Soul's Jazzie B., Mary J. Blige, David Bowie, Nicolas Cage, Luther Campbell, Al Capone, Jim Carrey, Morris Chestnut, Nat King Cole, Kim Coles, Crazy Legs, Bo Diddley, Taye Diggs, Christian Dior, Heidi Fleiss, George Foreman, Joe Frazier, John Galliano, Cuba Gooding, Jr., Grandmaster Flash, Ray J, LeBron James, Jam Master Jay, James Earl Jones, Roy Jones, Jr., Janis Joplin, Kid Rock, Martin Luther King, Jr., Eartha Kitt, Byron Lars, Stan Lee, Annie Lennox, Lisa Lisa, LL Cool J, Howie Long, Linda Lovelace, Susan Lucci, Marilyn Manson, Jesse L. Martin, Ricky Martin, Kate Moss, John Allen Muhammad, Dolly Parton, Elvis Presley, Raekwon, Hal Roach, David Ruffin, Sade, John Singleton, Slick Rick, Phil Spector, Howard Stern, Rod Stewart, Donna Summer, Verne "Mini-Me" Troyer, Tyrese, Darth Vader, Tiger Woods, Mia X, Sadat X, Denzel Washington

SOUL REBEL:

THE AQUARIAN OBSESSION
WITH FREEDOM IS
EXPRESSED WITH
PROPHETIC FLAIR BY THE
GREAT BOB MARLEY.

AQUARIUS 01.20–02.19

BACK TO THE LAB

masculine, *fixed, air*

Motto *I know*

Sound bite *"We refuse to be what you wanted us to be" (Bob Marley)*

Ruling planet *Uranus, Saturn*

Color *electric blue*

Rock *amethyst*

Physical *ankles, calves*

Icon *Jordan jumpman*

Genius *Bob Marley*

Beverage *Hypnotiq*

Guilty pleasure *breakin' it down*

Accessory *iPod*

Ride *Segway*

Find them *in the lab*

Visual 2001

THE RUNDOWN

Moment *Jordan taking off from the foul line*

Street occupation/grind *chemist, studio engineer, ménage à trois dealer*

Mix tape *Eric B. & Rakim, "Follow the Leader"; Dr. Dre, "Let Me Ride"; Bob Marley, "Natural Mystic"; Rick James, "Super Freak"; Cam'ron, "Horse & Carriage"; Bobby Brown, "My Prerogative"; Alicia Keys, "Fallin'"; Justin Timberlake, "Cry Me a River"; Shakira, "Whenever, Wherever"; D'Angelo, "Cruisin'"; Big Boi, "The Way You Move"; Phil Collins, "In the Air Tonight"*

Best-case scenario *Oprah Winfrey*

Worst-case scenario *Rick James, Bobby Brown*

Spot *Ethiopia*

Erogenous zone *airplane bathroom*

Vice *detachment*

Natural talent *overstanding*

Compatibilities *Aries, Gemini, Libra*

GHETTO INDEX

Gangstability	6	
Booty quotient	5	
Bling quotient	2	
Drama quotient	6	
Don status	7	
Trick status	4	
Game quotient	9	
Shiest quotient	7	
Freak quotient	8	

Aquarians are on a mission to save humanity. On some Buzz Lightyear shit. Sometimes, though, they're just on a mission. Few can fathom or really predict what Aquarians are about. What is guaranteed is that whatever it is will be that new, slightly off-center shit. What is not so guaranteed is how and in what form the new off-center shit will appear. Aquarians move in a swift, zigzag manner and can surprise you with a perspective out the clear blue sky. Like their symbol—the butt-nekkid man in the clouds pouring the waters of celestial knowledge out of an urn—they see things from above, peeping the pattern and passing on the information in innovative packaging. Like the two other air signs, Gemini and Libra, Aquarius trades in information and communication.

117

AQUARIUS

Usually the Aquarius is portrayed as a fey-looking man with a small pitcher, trickling out water like he's watering plants. That is not really the Aquarius story. If you want to see a tight rendering of the Aquarian symbol and you're ever in New York, the ceiling of Grand Central is more true to the Aquarian experience. The image is of a man struggling with a massive urn, and the water pouring out of it is not a trickle, it's floodwaters.

This combination of insight, ability to communicate, and a penchant to be on the next shit produces plenty of geniuses. Absentminded and scatterbrained though they may be, they are geniuses all the same. Many Aquarians are, in fact, visionary types and groundbreakers. Aquarian Oprah Winfrey, for example, created the formula for the successful talk-show format, inspiring endless copycats, none of whom could even come close to her level. She then branded herself and flipped her fame into restaurants, cookbooks, movies, a magazine, and a book club. Her approach to understanding people's problems and her sense of when and how to change her format and medium have made her a mammoth force in both television and publishing and placed her on the verge of becoming the first

black female billionaire. All the while, she breaks down doors for women (especially black women) and the downtrodden and overlooked. Shit, beat that with a bat.

Or consider "the God" of MCs, Rakim Allah. When the Aquarian MC stepped on

VISIONARY: OPRAH'S TREMENDOUS SUCCESS IS DEEPLY TIED TO HER HUMANITARIAN INSTINCTS.

the scene he changed hip-hop forever. There is before Rakim (Run-D.M.C.–styled exaggerated voices and hand gestures) and after (knowledge-based cool flow). With a lyrical style that evoked universality and science and a presence that was at once cool and deadly, Rakim laid down most of the style law for MCs today. At seventeen (!) he combined knowledge and conciseness with what writer Harry Allen once called "metaphor menace," creating the foundation for the definitive MC persona. Tupac, Wu-Tang, Jay-Z, Brand Nubian, Nas, Lauryn Hill, Mobb Deep, and countless others all owe him a debt.

Lastly, Aquarian sports legends like Jim Brown, Hakeem "The Dream" Olajuwon, Lawrence Taylor, and Wayne Gretzky transformed their sports from the moment they began to play professionally. Each had a style remarkable not so much for athletic prowess as for the drive and intelligence of their game. I mean, our man Olajuwon made the center position in basketball a lesson in graceful calculus; spinning, feinting, and using new angles to score sweetly from the big-man position. If you're into ball, a must-see is the NBA finals when Olajuwon schooled a much bigger and younger Shaq on the finer points of the down-low position. The Pisces Shaq came back next year less dependent on the smash dunk he had become so popular for, and added Olajuwonesque spins to his repertoire. But we digress.

Aquarian minds are in perpetual motion, whether working on a cure for nightmares, scheming on the next ménage à trois, or fiddling with their own perception of time. Basically, cats is stimulus-hungry. They live the life of ideas, moving quickly and Gemini-like from one possibility to the next. For the Aquarian, ideas are as real and tangible as bricks and asphalt. Still, most people ain't trying to hear that outer-space-nigga shit they be on. At first, anyway.

Blame it on the mad scientist disease (first cousin of mad cow) that infects many Aquarii. Folks are regular Dr. Frankensteins. Be all up

MAD SCIENTIST: AQUARIAN DR. DRE WAS THE MASTERMIND BEHIND SNOOP, EMINEM, N.W.A, AND 50 CENT.

in the lab concocting shit. Let us say here that it's a pretty safe bet that an Aquarian has a lab: an overcrowded place set aside for creation, examination, and experimentation. Not to mention a stash spot for their weed, et cetera. Let us also say that if an Aquarian is the get-high type, which many are, it's usually not escapist business like with some other signs in the zodiac (see Pisces); it's just giving their minds something else to do. Aquarian genius and superproducer Dr. Dre is drippin' with this particular aspect of the Aquarian persona. He, for one, dubbed himself Doctor. He is largely responsible for some of the wildest, most unlikely, and most successful pop concoctions in history: suburban favorites N.W.A, slit-eyed lanky gangsta icon Snoop Doggy Dogg, vehement and articulate white-trash poet Eminem. Add to that the fact that Dre celebrated lab-created marijuana on his multiplatinum album *The Chronic* and that on more than one occasion he dons the white lab coat in his video appearances. Mad scientist definitely. Doctor fa' sho. But a doctor of what?

Much more interested in tomorrow than today, Aquarians live in the future. This sometimes makes it difficult for people living in the here and now to relate to them. Hell, holding a conversation with these motherfuckers can twist a nigga up. Aquarians are just not interested in the status quo. They are a bit, uh . . . detached. "Touched" might be another way to put it. Like Buzz Lightyear, they walk around in astronauts' helmets, living according to their own rules and in their own atmosphere. Hence, Aquarians can be a little spacey. Evil-ass Aquarian Ronald Reagan ran the country thinking it was a movie set. He'd recall scenes from movies he'd starred in as if they actually happened in real life. Right before he'd make a speech, he would ask his assistant what his role was. Thing is, cat would get up behind the podium and bust it out. His sway over audiences was legendary.

Like the other two air signs, Gemini and Libra, Aquarius can take mind games to new levels. Dare to play with an Aquarian in the mental arena and you are liable to go crazy. Caution: they will blind you with science! Manipulate your sense of reality with dazzling new ways to break things down or turn things around. Aging player and actor Ice-T is a master at this; few artists have had so many lives and career options. The evil aspect of this air sign is that they can turn your life inside out just because they're bored and searching for something to mess with.

Experimenting is key. Always experimenting. This is at the root of their creativity. But some Aquarians take the experimenting shit too far. In the case of Rick James and Bobby Brown, that penchant for experimentation led them down the dark road of decadence. I mean, Rick James was in basements torturing chicks with crack pipes. This is what we call *taking things too far.* Ya know? And Bobby be getting arrested every other Tuesday on some jaywalking with prostitutes in

Texas puffin' on a blunt shit. Still, when on point, Aquarians are next level.

The experimentation continues into their sex lives. Sexually, Aquarians are ready to give themselves over to creation. Positions, textures, astral travel, candles, public places, what have you. Anything to increase the stimulation for the Aquarian. Rare is the Aquarian who is just pressed to hit it. The first and foremost thing for the Aquarian, male and female, is the mind. The attraction is mental first. Which is why it is mandatory for them to be friends first before they will hook up. They got to peep the mental state. "I push up like an exercise," Rakim once rhymed explaining how he approached women, "check the intellect and inspect the thighs." Aquarians fuck your mind. Masters of the mind fuck. But like Libras they can be too detached in bed, making you wonder, is homegirl/boy here with me or not?

Physically, Aquarians have a strange light in their face and eyes. Some sort of translucent light in the face. It's difficult to describe, but you can see it pretty clearly in the faces of Alicia Keys, Justin Timberlake, Brandy, even ugly-ass Chris Rock. It's hard to put your finger on it, but it is there.

Extra independent, they are loath to be tied down in any way, protecting their freedom at any cost. (Note: they will disappear on you!) They often rebel, like Aquarian James Dean. Freedom-loving to a fault, they maintain their independence and have an unusual ability to detach from the enslaving influence of emotions. Jealous lovers beware: trying to keep hold of Aquarius is like trying to slow the wind down. Pointless endeavor. Really. They value their independence over almost anything else and will protect it with all of their intellectual force. It is in the cause of freedom that they are particularly apt as leaders. Aquarian Angela Davis and her celestial afro became a defining image of the struggle for freedom and equality in the seventies. She inspired an entire generation to be themselves and to not accept oppression of any kind. The Honorable Robert Nesta Marley, a modern-day Aquarian prophet and a universally known and accepted icon for freedom fighters, not only wrote and performed songs that defined and demanded physical, mental, and spiritual freedom, he lived a life that expressed it in the most eloquent terms. He left a legacy that provided it for his children. He was the epitome of Aquarian principles of higher consciousness, freedom, and oneness of the human race.

In a different way, Michael Jordan came to represent freedom as well. The Jordan name and logo are modern Aquarian symbols, representing all that's good about Aquarius. Airborne alchemy, the highest aspirations, and on-the-fly creativity are balled up in one symbolic image. What Jordan was able to create with the basketball inspired an entire generation to become as intense and driven as he was.

There are two kinds of Aquarius, the Uranus Aquarius and the Saturn Aquarius, because they are ruled by both planets. The Uranus Aquarian is unpredictable and erratic, marked by sudden bursts of energy, inspiration, and creativity. They work almost by surprise. Their lives are disrupted by sudden, radical, lightning-quick changes and turnabouts. The Saturn Aquarian is more like the Capricorn in that there is no turning these cats from their kooky ideas.

That's their story and they're sticking to it. Ronald Reagan exemplified this sort, with his voodoo economics and evil-empire talk. He knew he was right, so there was no need to question it. The ironic thing is that the Saturn influence on Aquarians' personality makes them capable of getting stuck. Once they get on something they are loath to change, even when time and circumstances change. They hate to be wrong; even when everything is telling them that their revolution is over, they might get stuck promoting played-out concepts.

This stubbornness and blindness to change can be blamed on

the fact that the mind is strong drink for the soul but it ain't everything. But Aquarians maintain tight reins over their perceptions. An older Aquarian we'll call S. used to put it like this: "I see 'em and I don't see 'em." This ability to contour reality to their own whims serves them well but drives those close to them up the fucking wall. Aquarians often struggle with human emotion: all the weeping and mad gnashing of teeth does not compute. The women, in particular, are hard as steel, usually with eyes that sparkle with magnetic knowingness. Not a joke, Aquarian women. Not a game at all.

But if Aquarians are to evolve to the next level and live among the rest of humanity, they must get out of their heads. All the intellectual energy in the world cannot compete with love as a force. Intellectual-izing everything—failures, emotions, relationships—can be addictive. It removes one from the hard work of being in it and committing for real. Sometimes it makes for cold, unfeeling cats who cannot see what's really happenin'. Whas really good. Other times it creates a wall between Aquarius and everyone and everything else. The Aquarian lesson is balancing the mind with the heart.

THE INFAMOUS

Hank Aaron, Jennifer Aniston, Brandy, Bobby Brown, Helen
Gurley Brown, Jim Brown, LeVar Burton, Dick Cheney, Gary
Coleman, Phil Collins, Sam Cooke, D'Angelo, Stacey Dash,
Angela Davis, Geena Davis, James Dean, Dr. Dre, Thomas Edison,
Roberta Flack, Kirk Franklin, Wayne Gretzky, Arsenio Hall,
Sherman "George Jefferson" Hemsley, Florence Henderson,
Paris Hilton, Langston Hughes, Michael Hutchence, Ice-T, Rick
James, DJ Jazzy Jeff, Michael Jordan, Jim Kelly, Alicia Keys, Kim
Jong Il, Ashton Kutcher, Buzz Lightyear, Ed Lover, Lee Malvo, Bob
Marley, Chanté Moore, Toni Morrison, Paul Newman, Nick Nolte,
Noodles, Hakeem Olajuwon, Rosa Parks, Joe Pesci, Leontyne
Price, Rakim, Robert Redford, Jackie Robinson, Smokey
Robinson, Axl Rose, Johnny Rotten, Kelly Rowland, Babe Ruth,
Seal, Shakira, Jerry Springer, Lawrence Taylor, Justin Timberlake,
John Travolta, Alice Walker, Lucinda Williams, Oprah Winfrey,
Elijah Wood

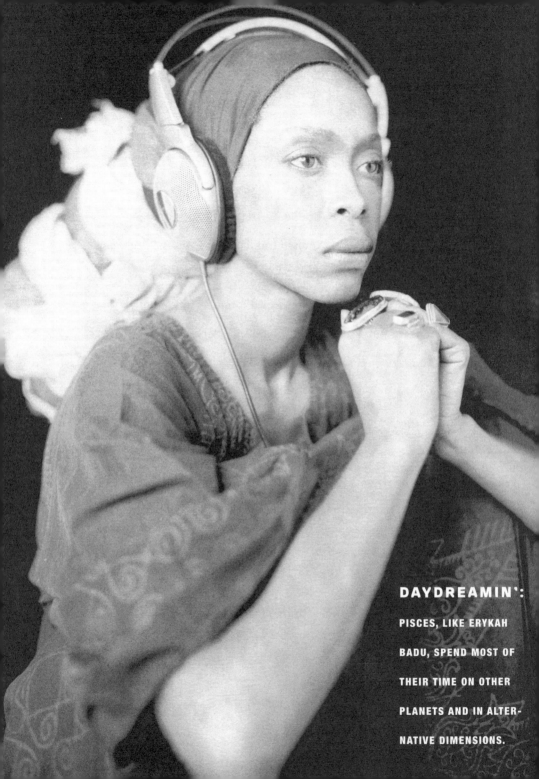

DAYDREAMIN':
PISCES, LIKE ERYKAH
BADU, SPEND MOST OF
THEIR TIME ON OTHER
PLANETS AND IN ALTER-
NATIVE DIMENSIONS.

PISCES 02.19–03.20

OL' SOULS

THE RUNDOWN

feminine, *mutable, water*

Motto *I believe*

Sound bite *"I guess I see ya next lifetime" (Erykah Badu)*

Ruling planet *Neptune*

Color *turquoise, pale green*

Rock *aquamarine, platinum*

Physical *feet*

Icon *Jesus*

Genius *Einstein*

Beverage *40-ounce of Olde English*

Guilty pleasure *having visions*

Accessory *throwback jersey, head wrap*

Ride *'64 Cadillac*

Find them *on the beach*

Visual Leaving Las Vegas

Moment *Jesus walking on water*

THE RUNDOWN

Street occupation/grind *addict, healing woman*

Mix tape *Nina Simone, "Sea Line Woman"; Method Man, "Bring the Pain"; Erykah Badu, "Next Lifetime"; Common, "The Light"; Queen Latifah, "Wrath of My Madness"; Nirvana, "Smells Like Teen Spirit"; Ja Rule, "Pain Is Love"*

Best-case scenario *Queen Latifah*

Worst-case scenario *Marion Barry*

Spot *Africa, prisons*

Erogenous zone *hot tub*

Vice *escapism*

Natural talents *rhythm, writing*

Compatibilities *Aquarius, Scorpio, Cancer*

GHETTO INDEX

Gangstability	4	
Booty quotient	7	
Bling quotient	2	
Drama quotient	7	
Don status	1	
Trick status	7	
Game quotient	6	
Shiest quotient	10	
Freak quotient	9	

Pisces ain't here to stay. As in here on Earth, that is. Strictly visiting. Folk got appointments. Be on other planets and shit. And they're late. Earth, for most Pisces, is just a waiting area to the next planet/dimension/vibration. And Pisces are generally none too thrilled to be here. They've had enough of this Earth business.

When funnyman Bernie Mac called out his two-year-old, bow-legged niece in *The Original Kings of Comedy* and exclaimed, "She bad! She a shepherd for the devil! This heifer been here before!," there's a good chance the child in question was a Pisces. Pisces are old souls, just finishing out their thousand-year bids on this planet. And so, from the time they are young, Pisces are exposed to information from the unconscious realm, remembering things from past lives, dreaming about conversations with dead relatives and walking with ghosts. They are often prodigies, mature for their age and highly capable of developing adult skills and techniques very quickly. Lil' Bow Wow is one example of the Pisces early starter.

Sensitive almost to a fault, Pisces feel and sense everything. A wide-open third eye is regular business for the Pisces. In the same way an entire school of hundreds of fish will all change direction at precisely the same time, the Pisces can read the vibe, sensing when something is about to jump off at a party. If you're in a club and Pisces gives you the "let's be out" signal, we suggest you follow it. That is, if these drunkards aren't bleary-eyed, rubbing up on some clownish-looking prospect for the evening. Knowing a Pisces is an unceasing reminder of the axiom "The Lord giveth and the Lord taketh away."

Sometimes all the "mystery" information granted to the Piscean soul is a little too much to handle. It can become a burden that no one understands. It's why that Pisces at the party might grab that bottle of Smirnoff for dolo—for self. (That's if they drink at all.) They're trying to drown out some of the voices. To escape that dark prison feeling that is the lot of all the water signs (Cancer and Scorpio being the others) but is extra intense in Pisces, the last of the group. (It's the sort of oppressive slow-moving feeling you feel when you're under water. Pisces, which represents the seas, often lives with the heavy pressure that exists in the deepest oceans.) Being high or drunk serves as temporary relief from the weight of being Mr. or Ms. Sensitivity.

KING OF PAIN: **CULT FIGURE, DRUG ADDICT, AND TORTURED GENIUS, KURT COBAIN LIVED A LIFE MARKED BY PISCEAN SELF-ANNIHILATION. HIS SONGS WERE INSIGHTFUL, POETIC, AND OFTEN HINTED AT SUICIDAL TENDENCIES.**

In their early years, Pisceans figure out pretty quick that they are kinda different from other kids and can quickly adjust to being alone if given something to occupy their imagination and exercise their quickly developing creative talents (writing stories, poetry, singing, acting, playing instruments, what have you). But they wear their sensitivity on their sleeve, making them open to getting teased, isolated, or bullied. This state of affairs often results in an accident-prone, shy, fragile, insecure child, who of course attracts even more problems. Still, the precariousness of their situation, along with all that isolation, gives Pisces early lessons in human nature and opportunities to explore themselves.

It's always kinda rough for Pisces. While some souls are still doing life's version of addition and subtraction, Pisces are doing trigonometry. Their lives are complex and difficult. By their own doing of course, so Pisces are highly susceptible to addictions, particularly drinking to handle the burdens. Because of this, many Pisces never drink, smoke, or do any drugs at all, already knowing the effect just one drink would have on them.

In their most evolved state, Pisces get Jesus-wit-it. (Nananana-nanaa!) To understand the entire Pisces complex, look to Jesus. Some people believe that the real-life Jesus was not born on December 25. That date comes from a pagan tradition called Saturnalia and has more to do with the equinox than the birth of the Christ child. No one really knows when the historical Jesus was born, but the figure in the Biblical mythos without a doubt represents Pisces. Look, he was surrounded on all sides by symbols of fish and water: the early Christian symbol was the fish, his disciples were fishermen ("I will make you fishers of men"), he was walking on water, feeding hordes with a couple bread loaves and fish nuggets. He made water baptism the new conversion style, and his was a life of sacrifice and high-frequency talk. (Typical Pisces traits.) Nobody fully understood him and he

walked the earth poor as a church mouse, preaching love, nonvio-
lence, sacrifice, and healing. If that ain't Pisces, we don't know what is.
His birth was the event that actually began the Piscean age, or the last
2,000 years of history. In the Bible, Jesus was a person who lived without judgment or sin but was persecuted and then crucified for, basically, keeping it real. He then became a symbol of the possibility of
human triumph over death and the material world. He returned from
the dead, and his soul completed the human cycle and ascended to
the higher dimensions. That, people, is where Pisces is. So forgive
them for their drunken trespasses; most are in the throes of an ongoing war for their souls. In fact, the astrological symbol of two fish
bound by the tail headed in opposite directions is an accurate por-
trayal of the ups and downs of the Piscean soul struggle.

That's why they sometimes seem distracted or slightly delu-
sional. Pisces gives you the impression of living outside of time and
space. Otherworldly. That *Baduizm*-type shit. This otherworldliness
can be real magical pixie-dust style, or it can be just plain fucking an-
noying. Erykah Badu is a classic example of the Pisces nature. Gifted
from the time she was a youngster in Texas, she came on the music
scene with an old juke-joint voice weighty with evocations from the
past: part Billie Holiday, part Nina Simone. Her look, with her large
dream-drenched eyes and angular body, is aquatic (especially when
she wore the oversized headdress), and her lyrics, costuming, and
stage presence (incense sticks, candles and color coordination,
crystals and sequencing) present a woman much concerned with
history and *vibration,* two languages Pisceans are rather fluent in.
The attention paid to our ancestors and to the silent frequencies that
surround us and guide our lives is why many Fishheads have psychic
abilities. These are folk who know even when they don't know. Everyone can benefit from keeping a journal of dreams, but Pisces would

OTHERWORDLY:
DESPITE HIS
ADDICTION, PISCEAN
HYPEMAN FLAVA
FLAV WAS A POP
ICON WITH A
BUGGED-OUT
PERSONA. MAD
CREATIVE, HE ALSO
PLAYED FOURTEEN
INSTRUMENTS.

particularly benefit. They have powerful dreams, which they value, and have an overactive subconscious.

Not to mention an overactive imagination. Because of this, they lie like a rug. The children lie about what they had for lunch. It's a particular challenge for them. For Pisces, especially when they are young, reality is something to play with and manipulate. Whereas Taurus children at the beach might be more attuned to the sensual pleasures of the sand and sea, Pisces children entertain themselves by building sand castles. This love of intangible dreams over material reality can develop into formidable talent or debilitating addiction. Or both. (Like the other dualistic sign in the zodiac, Gemini, Pisces juggles two or more personalities in one body.) Much depends on who and what a Piscean is surrounded by. Pisces Flavor Flav, the kitchen-clock-wearing voodoo hype man in Pub-

133

PISCES

lic Enemy and author of the phrase "Yeeeeeah boyeee," made headlines when it was discovered that he was addicted to crack. What few know about him is that outside of all the outrageous stage antics he is also an accomplished musician who can play fourteen instruments by ear.

Pisces are often crippled by the fear of ugly truths and their consequences. A Pisces might become paralyzed with fear at the prospect of telling his shortie about the phone calls they've been getting from an old flame. When said shortie ultimately finds out, the Pisces will come up with weak excuses as to why it wasn't mentioned. Unless particularly self-destructive or emotional, Pisces tend to flee from conflict, potential and otherwise, and would rather live with their delusions. When they lie, it's more self-deception than deception. They really want to believe what they are saying. (Their motto is: "I believe.") But Neptune, Pisces' planetary ruler, while gracing Pisces with a powerful imagination, also impairs the Piscean's perception of reality with pixie dust. The reality-on-the-ground usually conflicts with Neptune's illusions. That same hardcore Piscean faith/love/commitment can turn into a profound kind of denial/passive aggression/obsession, and on occasion a Piscean might get on some real stalker-type shit. Warning: if you sense stalker possibilities in a Pisces, it is time to MAKE MOVES. Get ghost! Bounce! Put a state or two between you. With a quickness! We mean it. Once committed, Piscean stamina for rejection is sky high. All the slammed doors, dial tones, crossin' streets to avoid them, what-part-of-no-do-you-not-understand lectures, and get-the-fuck-away-from-me's might not be enough. Seriously, the authorities might have to get involved. The Pisces faith, like the Leo will, is hard to break.

Resilient in many ways, Pisces folk sometimes grow to accept the excruciating pain and many obstacles that come with being advanced souls. Some Pisces get in touch with their compassion and use their experience and sensitivity to help and heal people. Others become victims of their sensitivity and self-destruct. Again, many do both. Jazzy-blues songstress Nina Simone converted her heartache from growing up young, dark-skinned, and female in the South during the period of civil rights and real-time Grand Dragon racism into voodoo protest songs. When you listen to songs like "Mississippi Goddam" or "Pirate Jenny," with their awkward, almost discordant piano and her sometimes strident vocals, it's like hearing the old obeah women from an ancient time and place casting deadly spells upon their enemies.

Physically, Pisces actually look like fish. Look at Pisceans Ja Rule, Erykah, Common, and Nina Simone closely and you can see the many and varied aquatic features. Some have huge watery eyes (Flavor Flav, or was it the high from crack?) that almost seem not to blink. Some have that sleek almost-dolphin look, their faces looking like they've been pulled back by tightly wound braids or headwraps. (In Ms. Badu's case, obviously, it actually is.) Or they have that whale look, sort of thick with small, knowing eyes and a large nose and mouth. And dilly or dull as they first seem, they are far more keen, far more wise than they appear. Mystery, usually propagated by their silence on certain matters, surrounds them.

But believe us, Pisceans know things. Their spiritual doors are wiiiiide the fuck open. So much so that drugs and drink only exacerbate an already iffy situation. These folk are so open that unless they're sturdied by other zodiac influences in their chart or by a strong spiritual background, they can be easily swayed and highly impressionable.

But there are benefits to being that open too, such as being excellent mimics and quick learners. A relationship with a Pisces can be like talking to a reflection. We knew a Pisces who had thirteen different personalities, one for each of the cliques she belonged to. With her family she was the quiet Japanese girl. With her thug boyfriend from Crooklyn she was the jaded drug moll slow-dragging a menthol. With her prep-school friends her accent took on Valley-girl intonations. While at her job she was Miss Professional. Her ability to pick up and project her surroundings was uncanny. One of the reasons Method Man became the first of the nine Wu-Tang Clan members to record a solo hit was that his style was a slick combination of all the Wu-Tang members around him. He took a piece of ODB, a piece of RZA, a piece of Raekwon, and a piece of GZA, creating a more universal style.

Mimicry is just one of many Piscean talents. But this fountain of talent is rooted in their fluency in vibration. In other words, rhythm. As yardies from Jamaica would say, *Dem people dey got some wicked riddim, ya see?* This

QUEEN, INC.: MANY PISCES, LIKE LATIFAH, ARE VERSATILE TALENTS, ADAPTABLE TO ALMOST ANY ENVIRONMENT.

highly developed rhythmic sense gives them skills. Dancing, writing, singing, massage, fucking—all in the Pisces repertoire. (We talkin' mind-expanding astral sex. Pisces, in fact, could vie for the title of most sexual zodiac sign. While the obvious choice, Scorpio, tends to have sex driven by ego needs and physical displays, Pisces wants to transcend the physical and use sex as a vehicle into other dimensions.) Think of the highly syncopated flow and gestures of the uberrhythmic Method Man, a.k.a. Tical. Or consider amphibian heartache-and-pain monger Ja Rule and how he pimped his innate sense of timing, pitch, and rhythm (and thuggish empathetic posture) into back-to-back-to-back platinum hits. Perhaps the best example in popular culture of how far the Piscean talent and versatility can be stretched is evolved Piscean Latifah. Blessed with an extravagance of talent, she has gone from pro-woman conscious rapper to singer to television and movie actress to talk-show host to highly successful businesswoman. And no matter what she creates on stage, wax, or screen, she retains an air of quiet wisdom about her, even when playing lesbian gangsters. Latifah is also a prime example of another type of voodoo the fish folk do. Get this: as they get closer to their natural age (see the discussion of the natural age of a sign in Aries, page 3), an ill kind of inversion takes place. These cats get younger as they get older. In some strange Neptunian twist, Pisces seem to get younger with age. Mature prodigious children seven decades later turn into spry and youthful elders. Go figure. It's a strange paradox.

All that to say the evolved Pisces is like the soul about to take off. As the fish folk get older and the physical becomes less and less a factor in their lives, Pisceans gain new confidence. If sufficiently evolved, Pisces begin to reap the rewards of a life of serious soul struggle. Knowledge, wisdom, and understanding manifest beauty and grace in their lives, and those who surround them begin to appreciate their value. The transition to the spirit world and death is not so great a leap for these folk. In fact, the evolved fish has been waiting for the day. Finally free to move about the universe. Finally free of the burdensome bag of flesh, blood, and bone. Finally free to hook up with Jesus and Tupac in dimension 360. Maybe discuss the finer points of sacrifice. Or whateverthefuck. END.

THE INFAMOUS

Desi Arnaz, Erykah Badu, Marion Barry, Drew Barrymore, Harry Belafonte, Osama bin Laden, Michael Bolton, Edie Brickell, Matthew Broderick, Les Brown, Irene Cara, Johnny Cash, Chilli, Chelsea Clinton, C-Murder, Kurt Cobain, Nat King Cole, Common, Billy Crystal, Benicio Del Toro, Fats Domino, Albert Einstein, Julius "Dr. J" Erving, Erik Estrada, Flavor Flav, David Geffen, Andy Gibb, Mikhail Gorbachev, Kelsey Grammer, Grand Puba, Jasmine Guy, Patty Hearst, Jennifer Love Hewitt, L. Ron Hubbard, D. L. Hughley, Ja Rule, Steve Jobs (creator, Apple), Quincy Jones, Jackie Joyner-Kersee, Queen Latifah, Spike Lee, Emmanuel Lewis, Lil' Bow Wow, Rob Lowe, Moms Mabley, Method Man, Christopher Moltisanti, Chuck Norris, Shaquille O'Neal, Wilson Pickett, Sidney Poitier, Freddie Prinze, Jr., Pat Riley, Kurt Russell, Dr. Seuss, Bugsy Siegel, Levi Strauss, Darryl Strawberry, Jimmy Swaggart, Elizabeth Taylor, Courtney B. Vance, Veronica Webb, Vanessa Williams, Bruce Willis, Nancy Wilson, Rod Woodson

Next Level

This book, of course, has to be taken with a grain of salt. As we said before, the preceeding chapters are just the tip of the iceberg. Sun signs are not the only influence on your personality. The moon, Mercury, and the other planets also influence your persona. People are always saying they doubt astrology because it is too general. Or that what most people describe as Leo doesn't actually describe you. And on some level this is probably true: the sun sign is a general description. And we have other influences affecting our demeanors. To get specific, you have to go further. We are talking about doing the birth chart.

The chart is the real breakdown—the real nitty-gritty. It is like a blueprint to the personality, a way of finding out everything from your sexual tendencies to how you spend your money to what your home life is like. It can give you a deeper understanding of your conflicts and why you may seem like one thing on the surface but be something entirely different beneath the surface. The rising sign, for example, influences how you appear to others. The moon, Mercury, and other planets also influence your person. The moon affects your emotions. Other important planetary influences are Venus, which speaks to how we love, and Mars, which speaks to how we fuck. Take Janet Jackson, for example. She is a Taurus sun sign, which gives her a sensual nature, big bovine eyes, and a talent for making money. But her moon is in Aries, which adds a fiery charge to her Taurean nature. So although Taurus is an earthy, slow-moving, and methodical sign, the Aries in her makes her bold, rash, and at times real rah-rah. Take an accounting of her emotional life and her quick-hit relationships and the Aries moon influence becomes quite apparent. And astrology can go much deeper and much further. To get a full picture of your astrological story, we recommend getting your birth chart done. All it requires is the time, date, and place you were born. You can get charts done over the Internet or you can contact us:

Zodiac Nation
174 Nassau Street
Brooklyn, NY 11201

or log on to www.zodiacnation.com

Acknowledgments

God.

Spiritual family: Hildegarde Yvonne, Uncle Joe, Arayna Bazard, Eulice Rodriguez, Mozell Haynes.

Magett family: Stephen, Leonardo, Mozell, David, Gwen, Stephanie, Elijah, Rashad Smith, Shalima, Catherine.

Extended: Audrey, Keronda, and Elliott family; Ming, Randy, and Phillips family; Tisha, Tamara, and Luckett family; Dolores and Pate family.

Super support: Takisha Olugbolagun, Athena Cross-Edge, Alejandro Bradley, Alexander Allen, Gwen Wunderlich.

Sistren: Susan Moses, Julia Chance, Kierna Mayo, Joicelyn Dingle, Aretha Sarfo, Raquel Cepeda, original *Honey* crew.

The ever-patient editor Melody Guy and Daneille Durkin.

Literary agent extraordinaire Tanya McKinnon and Mary Evans.

Legal eagles Erika Munro, Tamayu Takayama, and Nova Perry.

Photo assistant Kali Abdullah. George Pitts and Duane Pyous.

Barron Claiborne, Jonathan Mannion, Michael Benabib, Caroline Torem-Craig, Jerome Laguierre, Glen Elf, Sharon Washington.

Emilio "Stretch" Austin, Jr., for pushing me to pursue a career in fashion and mag publishing in the first place.

—S.M.

Thanks to God, Odumare, Sibi, Kimica Carey, Donna Blair, Richie Carey, Kawima, Patricia Peters, Christopher Brown, Tony Brown, the Lawson family, the Marriott family, Khem, Niko, Taiye, Kimani, Karif and Lorna Marriott, Claudette Clovey, Beverly and Stephanie and the entire Smith family, Nnenna Onyiwuchi, Ashleigh Roberts, Sagal Abshir, Herb Raynaud, Reggie Dennis, James Bernard, Darryl Dawsey, my agent Tanya McKinnon, Mary Evans, the ever-patient Melody Guy, Danielle Durkin, Barron Clairborne, Jerome Laguierre, Glen Elf, Dustin Millman, Dreu Pennington-McNeil, Tracy Funches, Michael Benabib, Michael Ochs, Feckson Ngoma, Helen Shelton, Roberta Magrini, Audrey, Natasha, Kanyasu, Bradford Muchila, Monica, Bene, Arshud, Begay, Rome, Don Ruff and family, Michaela Angela Davis, and Raquel Cepeda.

—R.M.

Photo Credits

Grateful acknowledgment is made to the following for permission to reprint photographs contained in *Astrology Uncut:*

page xvi: © Michael Ochs Archive.com

page xvii: © Michael Ochs Archive.com

page xviii: © Bettmann/CORBIS

page xix: © Wilfredo Lee/Getty Images

page xxii: © Jason Kirk/Getty Images

page 2: © Jerome Laguierre

page 5: © Paramount Pictures/Getty Images

page 8: © Michael Ochs Archive.com

page 9: © Vince Bucci/Getty Images

page 12: © Adger Cowans/Blackimages

page 15: © Michael Ochs Archive.com

page 17: © Reuters NewMedia Inc./CORBIS

page 22: © Michael Ochs Archive.com

page 27: © Jerome Laguierre

page 29: © Raymond Boyd/Michael Ochs Archive.com

page 30: © Caroline Torem-Craig

page 32: © CORBIS

page 38: © Jerome Laguierre

page 39: Courtesy of Atlantic Records

page 42: © Brenda Chase/Getty Images

page 45: © Arnaldo Magnani/Getty Images

page 48: © Anthony Barboza/Blackimages

page 50: © Michael Ochs Archive.com

page 54: © Frank Micelotta/Getty Images

page 58: © Michael Ochs Archive.com

page 60: © Michael Ochs Archive.com

page 62: © Michael Benabib

page 66: © Getty Images

page 71: © Gary M. Prior/Getty Images

page 73: © Robert Mora/Getty Images

page 78: © Barron Claiborne

page 82: © Tracy Funches

page 83: © Mark Mainz/Getty Images

page 86: © Jonathan Mannion

page 90: © Stuart Franklin/Getty Images

page 95: © Michael Ochs Archive.com

page 96: © Michael Ochs Archive.com

page 99: © Al Pereira/Michael Ochs Archive.com

page 102: © Barron Claiborne

page 106: © Michael Ochs Archive.com

page 108: © Robert Sengstacke/Blackimages

page 110: © PACHA/CORBIS

page 114: © Michael Ochs Archive.com

page 118: © Mark Mainz/Getty Images

page 120: © Frederick M. Brown/Getty Images

page 126: © Barron Claiborne

page 130: © Michael Ochs Archive.com

page 133: © Michael Ochs Archive.com

page 136: © Getty Images

Rob Marriott is a twelve-year veteran of music journalism and author of *Pimpnosis.* He has written for *New York* magazine, *Essence, Rolling Stone, Vibe, Spin,* and *The Source.* He won the ASCAP–Deems Taylor Award for excellence in music journalism for his coverage of the death of Tupac Shakur for *Vibe.* He served as editor of *The Source* and was a founding editor of *XXL.* He lives in Brooklyn, New York, and Zambia, Africa, with his wife and daughter.

Sonya Magett has worked in magazine publishing and entertainment for ten years; she began fresh out of high school. She is recognized as a preeminent stylist and fashion editor, having worked for or with *The Source, Vibe, Rolling Stone, Mode,* and BET.com. She was the launching fashion editor for *Honey* magazine. Among the celebs she has styled: OutKast, Maxwell, Tyra Banks, Lauryn Hill, Mary J. Blige, Lil' Kim, Destiny's Child, Erykah Badu, Notorious B.I.G., and LL Cool J. She is currently a style director at a new women's magazine from Time Inc. and at *Essence* magazine. She lives in Brooklyn, New York.